4th and Long
The Odds

4th and Long
The Odds

✦

MY JOURNEY

Sean Stellato

iUniverse, Inc.
New York Lincoln Shanghai

4th and Long The Odds
MY JOURNEY

iUniverse books may be ordered through booksellers or by contacting:

iUniverse
2021 Pine Lake Road, Suite 100
Lincoln, NE 68512
www.iuniverse.com
1-800-Authors (1-800-288-4677)

ISBN-13: 978-0-595-34231-0 (pbk)
ISBN-13: 978-0-595-67080-2 (cloth)
ISBN-13: 978-0-595-79001-2 (ebk)
ISBN-10: 0-595-34231-0 (pbk)
ISBN-10: 0-595-67080-6 (cloth)
ISBN-10: 0-595-79001-1 (ebk)

Printed in the United States of America

To Mom and Dad, my role models and true best friends. Words cannot describe what you mean to me. Thanks for teaching me not to let anyone discourage me from chasing my dreams and to stay humble. To Eric and Michael the best older brothers a younger brother could want. From day one you both have been role models in your own way that helped lay the foundation down to get started on my journey. To Krista Lantych, for making tremendous sacrifices that enabled me to go fulfill my dreams. You have had a profound impact on my life and are a "Dream come true" best friend and partner in life. In addition for helping me restructure and edit this book. She also helped me recall the positive experiences in my life helping me see everything that I have achieved. To my Aunt Laurie and cousin Nicole for the good times we shared. To Ron Jones, the best personal trainer a player could have, your generosity, guidance and expertise played a pivotal role in my success; to my Owa, Lillian Stellato, you have been my true inspiration and I know you will always be with me. Shirley 'Nana' Destefano, for creating such a special mom in my mother, I love you. To my nephews Michael Jr, Vincent and Troy may someday I impact your lives the way your fathers have done to mine; to Jody Ryan a friend who passed well before his time, thanks for teaching me to appreciate life. Mike Lovett the best damm sports therapist in the business, you enabled me to master workouts. To Howie Olson, my Pop Warner C-Team coach for helping me hatch from my shell and play with complete confidence. Chris Carroll for your wise advice and friendship. To John and Cathi Lantych thanks for your support and raising such a special daughter. Gena Lantych for always being there for me to help complete this book. Ken Perrone thanks for believing in me. To the dreamer; may you continue to dream and stay focused at all times or you will be chasing your dream all night. And to every kid who has a dream don't let anyone ever discourage you from fulfilling it, never give up. With a vision, you're well on your way. To God for being my faith that keeps me going and helped guide me to live a righteous life-SS. God-Bless

Contents

CHAPTER 1   DEDICATION TO THE GAME 1

CHAPTER 2   WARM UP 3

CHAPTER 3   RUN AS FAST AS YOU CAN 9

CHAPTER 4   SCALE SAYS SIXTY-FIVE POUNDS 13

CHAPTER 5   CRUSADER OR WITCH 18

CHAPTER 6   FLYING WITCHES 23
              WITCH HUNT

CHAPTER 7   OWA GUIDANCE FROM ABOVE 29
              TURNOVER

CHAPTER 8   THE GUNNERY FIRST & LONG 33

CHAPTER 9   MARIST COLLEGE RED FOXES SAFETY 52

CHAPTER 10   RENEWED INSPIRATION 58

CHAPTER 11   SPEED KILLS! SURVIVAL OF THE
              FASTEST 61

CHAPTER 12   MY FOURTH QUARTER 66

CHAPTER 13   FINAL DRIVE 75
              OVERTIME

CHAPTER 14   POLITICS & CHANGES IN FOOTBALL IN
              THE PAST 30 YEARS 85

CHAPTER 15   THE FORTY-YARD DASH: $$ 93

CHAPTER 16   IRON MAN FOOTBALL: INSIDE THE
ARENA 95
CHAPTER 17   LIFE IT'S OKAY TO DREAM 103
4th AND INCHES

1

DEDICATION TO THE GAME

"When someone tells you that you can't go any further, just tell them to look behind you and see how far you've come."

—Anonymous

As I got dressed for senior day November 17, 2001 for the last time in my Marist College football uniform I got severe chills. Moments later I looked myself in the mirror and promised myself this would not be the last time I put on a football uniform. The last football game at Marist College was extremely emotional for me. This day represented that I had defied the odds and played four years of Division I football. However I wanted more. I had a passion for the sport and wanted to go beyond everyone's wildest dreams. I wanted to go pro.

I felt at ease playing in my last game at Marist College knowing that my parents along with my girlfriend would be taking the road trip that they had made numerous times before to see me play. My parents always made it quite apparent that if I were playing in China, they would make arrangements to come to the game. I cannot recall a time that my parents were not in the stands cheering for me. My father Patrick Stellato first started videotaping me in 1985 when I started playing Pop Warner at the age of seven. As the years passed and technology became more advanced so did my father's equipment. My mother Gloria Stellato has been my number one cheerleader since I first stepped on the field. She went as far as painting my number on her face and wearing a pin with my football picture. My girlfriend, and future wife Krista Lantych, was always there to support me and has stood by me through thick and thin. I had two older brothers back home in Massachusetts. Even though they could not make it to a lot of my college games they had a way of making me feel that I was close at heart. My oldest brother Michael was just starting his family making it hard for him to take the long drive. My other brother Eric came to as many games as his job would allow. They both made it a habit to contact me before I stepped on the field and coached me up for each game.

During the Thanksgiving break from college in 2001, my father and I reminisced about the past sixteen years of football. It was then I revealed that I wanted to go after my life long dream to go pro. Gratefully my parents and Krista supported my decision. My father and I put together a blueprint on how we would go about marketing myself for the professional teams. The day after Thanksgiving, my father and I spent sixteen hours breaking down film and finding the most impressive highlights. The highlight film that we created was ten minutes in length and contained segments from my college career. We sent these tapes out with a trading card that had an action photo on one side, and my vital statistics on the reverse side. In addition, I enclosed a letter giving a brief summary about myself as well as my contact information. We mailed out a tape to every Arena team, a few Arena 2 teams (the developmental league for Arena) and several Canadian League teams.

About twenty-two tapes were mailed out all over the country, ranging from Estero, Florida to Los Angeles, California. The NFL draft was never considered a realistic option due to the fact that Marist never held pro days or had scouts come to see the players. The next month or so was a very nerve racking experience waiting for some sort of positive feedback. In the meantime it was time for me to finish up my final semester and continue working on every aspect that was related to excelling in football. The Marist College chapel was a very common place for me. I prayed daily for my loved ones and asked God to lead me in the right direction. My only question was would my prayers for playing professional football ever be answered?

2

WARM UP

"Whenever you start-give it your best. The opportunities are there to be anything you want to be. But wanting to be someone isn't enough; dreaming about it isn't enough; thinking about it isn't enough. You got to study for it, work for it, fight for it with all your heart & soul, because nobody is going to hand it to you."

—General Colin Powel

Statistics show that less then 10 percent of people who buy a book read past the first chapter. (Awaken The Giant Within, by Anthony Robbins) You made it past the first chapter. Good start, your in the upper percentile. Stay focused and motivated.

My family has always lived along the coast in Massachusetts. There are pieces of Stellato history all over the Boston area. My father spent the first nineteen years of his life in Somerville, which is located right next to Boston. My beautiful mother grew up in a neighboring city in Chelsea, and spent some of her childhood in Revere. After my parents tied the knot they lived in Revere. While living in Revere they were trying to save money and to find the perfect spot to raise their family. Almost a decade later my parents decided to raise their family just twenty minutes north of Boston in historic Salem, Massachusetts.

My parents met the way many Bostonian teenagers of their generation did, while doing their best imitations of Fred Astaire and Ginger Rodgers on the dance floor at the Italian/American club in Everett. My father was eighteen and just received an honorable discharge from the Navy. My father's dad, Pasquale was dying from Leukemia, this was a very tough time for him because his mother was also struggling financially. During this heartbreaking time my father got a job and gave his mother his entire paycheck. This alone tells me how family-ori-

3

ented a man my Dad is and raised his family to be the same. I cannot ever image where I would have ended up without the guidance of my father. He has had a profound impact on my life. My Dads father Pasquale came from the old country. He had very little education but still managed to raise two families. This is a man I wish I had the opportunity to meet and I consider a great man.

At the time when my parents first met, my mother Gloria had just graduated from high school. As the story goes, apparently they were making eye contact all evening but neither of them would make the first move. Finally my soft-spoken mother gave in and approached the dark haired Italian Stallion; she said "I guess I would be waiting all night if I waited for you to ask me to dance." My mother gave him her number at the end of the night and told him she was leaving for a week to go to Florida with her mother. To make a long story short, my father got a severe throat infection that lingered for weeks and didn't call. A few weeks later they ran into each other and the rest is history.

Both of my parents had very tough upbringings and simply amaze me each day with the unconditional love they show. My mother Gloria's father left when she was only five. Her father never gave her mother any child support for the three children he abandoned. My mother grew up in complete poverty but was surrounded by unconditional love from her mother. Her mother had to work two jobs to barely get by. When my mom was 10 her mother Shirley remarried. They moved to Revere to live with her stepfather's family. While living in Revere one night when the entire family was sleeping, her step Uncle Joe DeStefano plotted to murder the family and had a bullet for each person. Joe entered his brother's room in the middle of the night and shot his brother in the chest. At that time Shirley was pregnant with my Aunt Laurie, as he attempted to shoot the gun at her it jammed. Seconds later, Gloria, my Aunt Elaine, and my Uncle Stevie ran into the room, seeing this evil person hitting their mother with the barrel of the gun. All three children attacked the intruder, and through this courageous act, disarmed Joe. Gloria's stepfather died three-month's later from a gunshot wound; fortunately Shirley physical suffering was limited to a broken arm. However the entire family suffered from the stress it caused. They had no place to live during this period until Bruno's, a funeral home in Revere, put them up in their home for a month. Joe DeStefano, the alleged shooter with premeditated intentions to murder the entire family was acquitted for the reason of insanity. This story sends chills through my body, and scares my mother tremendously to this day. It saddens me that my mother went through this at such a young vulnerable age. It is amazing the woman that she became after going through so much hardship as a child. I guess my grandmother's love and devotion helped my mother develop into a wonderful giving person.

Patrick and Gloria wed on September 9, 1961. Early on, my parents struggled to make ends meet. Patrick worked two jobs: Laboratory for Electronics, (LFE), and Filenes. Gloria was a bookkeeper at John Hancock in Boston. She stopped working in 1964 when she became pregnant with Michael, who was born in November of 1965. They resided in a small apartment in Revere, Massachusetts until 1969. After spending a year looking for a house, they found an affordable one located in Witchcraft Heights in Salem, Massachusetts. It was the perfect spot for them to raise their family, it was not only affordable but it was also considered a safe family neighborhood. Witchcraft Heights is located near Gallows Hill, which is where all the so-called witches were hung and pressed to death during the Salem Witch Trials of 1692.

Eric was born in March of 1973, Patrick and Gloria had decided that Michael and Eric would complete the Stellato clan, but little did they know what was in store for them several years later. My parents were very surprised when my mother found out she was pregnant with me. They always believed that things happen for a reason. When I was born my Aunt Laurie did not know I was a boy and started asking the nurse if they had run out of pink blankets. When the nurse revealed my sex, she started crying. I heard she cried for a week straight. Gratefully her prayers were answered a few years later when she gave birth to my cousin Nicole in the summer 1981.

Many things changed for the Stellato family on August 21, 1981. This was supposed to be a very happy day, because it was my father's birthday. Instead, there was tremendous grief. It was devastating. My maternal grandmother Shirley DeStefano, passed away unexpectedly at the young age of sixty. This left a decision for my parents to make that would affect the entire Stellato family. My grandmother, Lillian Owa Stellato lived in Revere with my Aunt Laurie, and my newborn cousin, Nicole. They were financially unstable, so my parents invited them to move into our home in Witchcraft Heights. My paternal grandmother moved into our house. At the same time my Aunt Laurie and cousin Nicole moved into my brother Michael's room. That meant that I would share a room with both my brothers Eric and Michael. My brothers had the bunk beds, and I got stuck with a small cot. I am still a little sour due to the fact that I spent ten years sleeping on a cot, which gave me lower back problems. However I would not trade those ten years of us sharing that room for anything. The bond that was created and the respect that we developed for each other continues to grow as time goes by. By living with my Aunt Laurie and cousin Nicole I learned that they would always have my back and do anything for me. I also had the opportunity to grow up with my cousin Nicole, which was like having a younger sister.

Even though there is a tremendous age difference between my bothers and I, we found ways of bonding with each other. Growing up, all three of us idolized certain celebrities. I pretended that I was Don Johnson, Eric was John Travolta, and Michael was Sylvester Stallone. We all were told that we resembled them a little. The funny thing was that Eric used to sleep with his finger sticking in his chin trying to get the dimple that John Travolta had; surprisingly it never worked. When it was time for bed instead of getting put to sleep to the adventures of Peter Pan and Three Blind Mice, my father would reminisce about the Celtics glory years with the likes of Russell, Cousy, and some guy that stole the ball named Havlicek. My father's earliest jobs were selling newspapers at the Boston Garden when the Celtics started building one of the greatest sports legacies ever.

There was seldom lack of love or laughter in our household. We realized at a young age that those were vital ingredients for a wonderful life. That's how it was when we first entered the world and that is the same way I will bring up my family some day. No matter how many things changed or how many different avenues our lives might take, that is how our family will always be.

The two greatest assets that my family has helped me develop are my commitment and work ethic. My work ethic is a quality that my parents and grandparents instilled in me at an early age. My father worked two jobs for eleven years straight, often working up to ninety-five hours a week. My mother defines the all around perfect homemaker and gives it a new meaning. I would like to see other housewives keep up with her; she is simply amazing. My grandmother Owa worked until the ripe old age of eight-five, before retiring. She was no stranger to hard work. I recall finding it odd that my friend's grandparents didn't work and wondered what they did all day. My family's work ethics tell a great deal about their makeup. They display a type of drive that the average person is a stranger to. My parents always made sure that they could not only provide us with the toys and clothes we wanted but always ensured that they provided us with all the love and support we needed. Through this they have laid down a foundation that has enabled their children to understand that it is okay to bend, but never to break. They also have always stressed the importance of relying on intuition. My parents, like myself, have truly believed in order to be successful you must be more productive today than you were yesterday. That is a motto that I live by. They have been instrumental in my development as a person as well as an athlete. My parents are my inspiration as well role models and I am simply blessed to have them as my parents. I realize the majority of people will say that they have the "best" parents in the world, but I feel that I really do.

Salem is a good size blue-collar community in Northeastern Massachusetts along the coastline. It is the home to many different ethnic backgrounds, ranging from French, Italian, Irish and Hispanic. It is over eight square miles and has a population of around 39,250. It is only about eighteen miles north of Boston, but is much different in terms of lifestyle. Certain parts are lower middle class while others are upper middle class. It is a city where if you have your own vision or sights set on something, you have to work hard for it and be able to stand up for yourself. The city relies on tourism as a major source of revenue. Halloween in Salem is equivalent to New Years Eve in Times Square. Witchcraft hysteria fills the streets of Salem every October 31st.

Growing up my house was average size with three bedrooms and two baths. The backyard was big enough to have some serious games with the neighborhood kids. We had a small in-ground pool, which was for the most part a blast, except for when the Marco Polo games went bad. Often my mother found me running up the back stairs crying because Michael used me as a decoy and caused me to get water up my nose. At a young age, Michael instilled in me a competitive attitude. Therefore I became a complete perfectionist. This has stuck with me, and I believe that is why I am such a fierce competitor and never settle for ordinary. From a young age I have lived by the words, "Average is not an option, and you only live once."

The neighborhood was a blast filled with excitement and friends. I don't recall ever being bored as a child; there was always something to do and someone to play with. The elementary school, "Witchcraft Heights", I attended, as a child was located right behind my house. It had a basketball court, baseball field, and a park with a playground. We played it all, from hide and go seek, street football, basketball, and whiffle ball. I had friends my own age however I loved to tag along with my brothers and to be part of their crowd. I was involved in intense games at a young age with much older children. This got me into trouble at a young age of five when I severely broke my wrist. It was a snowy night in November and that meant that the neighborhood kids would have competitive tackle street football games on lightly covered cement pavement. This meant that it was time to do my best impressions of my favorite football player, Walter Payton. The object was to use the snow banks on the side of the street when you were going to get tackled. This night I did, but there was a fire hydrant lightly camouflaged with snow. I got tackled on it and broke my wrist. To make matters worse, it didn't heal correctly and I had to have it re-broken without anesthesia due to the fact that my parents were skeptical of anesthesia and decided to play it safe. My mother said that when the doctors re-broke it, I did not let out a peep and kept a straight face. I guess that was the moment I knew that I had a high threshold for pain and that football was the sport for me.

I really had no fears as a kid: roller-skating through stop signs, jumping off school roofs, walking on ponds with thin ice, sliding down high hills, or running into parked cars playing football. I feel one of my strongest assets, as a football player, is my versatility, which I credit in part to those street football games. In addition to my fearless behavior as a child, pool hopping was another daring thing we used to do. This consisted of jumping in and out of pools in the neighborhood in the pitch black and running not to get caught. Every summer this was exciting and it helped work on developing my fast twitch muscles.

Since I was the youngest out of the neighborhood crew, instead of not only developing friendships I also found role models and tried to be like them. To this day I am not sure if some of them realized it, and I question if I should have ever let them know. One of the neighborhood kids as well as my brother's friend Rob Cornell was an athlete I tried to follow growing up. Rob was a very skilled athlete and always had time for me, which made me feel like I belonged with the older crowd. His life ended this past Christmas night almost directly behind my bedroom window.

3

RUN AS FAST AS YOU CAN

"You've got to get up every morning with determination if you're going to go to bed with satisfaction."

—Anonymous

My parents saw my natural athletic ability when I was six years old. I was playing in my first organized basketball game. My father told me that I showed the ability to play the game of basketball at a higher level than my peers, and from that point on I played at a higher level. I attribute this to the fact that I had two older brothers that I some how managed to keep up with. I viewed my brothers as role models and learned from them. As a child I was always on the go and was filled with endless energy that amazed my parents. I had so much energy as a child; there was no stopping me. The same goes today and my co-workers are amazed by my endless supply of energy. The thought that I could not do anything because of my size or age never entered my mind. I never used my size as a crutch; instead I used it as a positive, and believed it only made me stronger and faster. I learned at a young age, that I could achieve anything if I put my mind to it.

I first realized I had a God given talent when I was in the first grade. My favorite game in gym class was called "cars". The game was played with twenty-five to thirty kids. The gym teacher was Dave Wilber and he had a way of making gym class fun. He was also an assistant football coach at Salem High School. He was very energetic and encouraging to all his students. He would pick one student that would be a cop and put them at half court, the rest of the students would get numbers and a car name such as Lamborghini, Ferrari, Porsche, and Corvette. Mr. Wilbur would call out a name of a car and it was off and running. As students got tagged they would become cops and eventually outnumber the cars.

Mr. Wilbur used to tell me that I was fast and encouraged me to me run as fast as I could. Those words became programmed into my head and I kept them close to me when I played any sport or game. I used to love it when ten kids would come at me and I had to juke left, right, and dive or slide over the line. I would do almost anything to avoid getting tagged and I carried this attitude onto the football field. I used to go home from gym class with floor burns and cuts. I guess it was getting me ready to play on the brutal artificial turf.

I also enjoyed dodge ball during gym class. It's scary to think back at it because I used to try to hit all my classmates in the face. I did this because my brothers used to get me so angry; since I was so much younger and smaller than them I just couldn't retaliate. So while I was playing dodge ball I would pretend that all the kid's faces were my brothers and fire away. My brother Michael used to hold me down when I came home form the orthodontist and had my braces tightened. He would poke at my sore teeth until I started to scream. At home I used to antagonize my brothers so much that they would come at me and try to catch me. Just like in football, when there are eleven maniacs coming after you once you get the ball that want to tackle you, my brothers wanted to get me. I would try to shake them and avoid being caught by them, however it seldom worked. My strategy was that if I could try to escape them that it would better prepare me for the game "cars" because they were much bigger and stronger than anyone in my gym class.

Starting in second grade, kids used to challenge me before school to race, but it was seldom I found any real challengers. Anytime a new student arrived at school, there was always talk about whether he would be able to beat me in a race. All through elementary school, I never lost a race. Trust me, I am no Maurice Green but people say that I can move for a white guy.

I used to tease my father and tell him that I got all my athletic ability from my mother's side of the family. My mother took competitive acrobatic dance classes as a child at the Veronica Zunino Dance Studios. Her picture appeared in the Boston paper when she preformed in the *Stars of Tomorrow*. She was very talented and extremely limber. She used to be able to do a bridge and drink a class of water while remaining upside down. This has always fascinated me and I longed to be as flexible as her to help me with my speed and agility.

The first organized sport my parents signed me up for was soccer when I was five years old. Even though I only played this sport for a few years it contributed greatly to my success as a field goal kicker. Another sport my parents signed me up for was basketball. I was in the "Cartoon League" in Salem, which consisted of elementary school children. I instantly fell in love with the sport and I could not get enough of it. Games were only every Saturday morning; it simply was not enough for me. Since my brothers and I had so much energy my parents wanted us to channel it into our academics and sports. So my father cut down a giant tree next to the house and paved over the grass to put up a hoop. It may sound like he was trying to copy Kevin Costner in *Fields of Dreams,* but nonetheless over the years I was very fortunate to have a great deal of success playing basketball. My father jokes with me that I used to dribble the ball with two hands and that is why he had to put up the hoop, we both know that's not true.

One of my closest childhood friends, Justin Kingston, deserves some credit for my success in sports. Justin was the type of friend that would drop everything if I needed him to shag balls or run patterns and catch the football. He helped me improve as an athlete.

The first year I played basketball I played well and many thought that I should have been awarded rookie of the year, but I didn't receive the award. I remember crying for a day straight. It was not that I felt that I was better then anyone else, it was because of the time and effort that I put into the sport. I improved my game and won league M.V.P the following season. It was hard for me not to keep a chip on my shoulder from the first season. Gratefully my brother Michael helped me over come that period in my life.

Baseball was another sport in which I had a great deal of success in while growing up. I played from the minor leagues all the way up to my sophomore year in high school. Many family members felt this would have been the sport that would be my best chance to get to the professional level. I played every position on the baseball team, but my best spots were center field and pitcher. My brother coached me in Little League, from the minor league to major league.

Mike took me under his wing and helped me develop into one of the premier younger athletes in the area. Mike was like a father figure to me when I was younger. My father traveled a great deal with his job and was not around much. Mike used to take me everywhere and we usually did something sports related. When other kids were vacationing at Disney or other exotic places I was at either football or basketball camp. Michael's commitment to my career served as a key component in me becoming a professional athlete. I know that we have had a major impact on each other's lives.

The only time it wasn't fun to have Mike as a coach, was when I wasn't focused or when we lost the game. He was always behind me through thick and thin. When I was eleven I was playing in the city championship and Mike was my coach. It was a very close game thanks to the umpire. Towards the end of the game, there was a really bad call, and something came over me. I guess I watched too much George Brett as a kid. I ran at the umpire and told him he sucked, and got ejected. Moments later my brother Mike went nuts on both umpire's and he too got ejected. The next night, we both watched our team lose from the stands. I learned a great deal from that experience, and never made that mistake again.

When I was young my father was a chain smoker, and boy did it bother me. I wanted him around when I was older and I was determined to make him quit. My dad's father passed away when my dad was a teenager, and I didn't want anything to happen to my father. I knew how detrimental cigarettes were to the human body and was scared that I would lose my father at a young age if he didn't quit. I had a stack of hopes and dreams that I wanted to fulfill, and I wanted him to be around to enjoy every step of the way with me. As the story goes, I used to do every conceivable thing to try and get him to quit, from taping my picture on the carton to cutting his cigarettes in half. He just would not quit. One day he said "Sean, if you pitch a no hitter, I will quit smoking." From that day on, I was determined; I was going to make him quit. It was a hot summer day, and I played for the Little League Yankees, and we were playing the Reds. My dad was standing in center field, this game I was in the zone, it was the bottom of the sixth inning and I made eye contact with him. He was sweating like Chevy Chase was when he was stranded in the desert in National Lampoons Vacation. I struck out the first two batters and the next batter hit a blooper over the second basemen's head and it was over. I turned around and my father lit up a cigarette right in center field, I was devastated. My father eventually gave up smoking in 1992, and he feels it was one of the most positive things he has ever done.

4

SCALE SAYS SIXTY-FIVE POUNDS

"Be more concerned with your character than your reputation, because your character is what you really are, while your reputation is merely what others think you are."
—John Wooden

I will be forever grateful that my parents got me involved in sports at a young age. Instead of hanging out on the street at night and up to no good, I was either at a game or practicing. Football structured my life and brought my family and I tremendous joy. I enjoyed every sport as a child however when I stepped onto the football field it was then my spirit was lifted. Even today when I step on the field my worries are forgotten and the joy of the game lifts my soul.

When I was in the second grade I watched my brother Eric excel in Pop Warner Football. His talent amazed me and I wanted to play, I wanted to be just like my older brother. When I was seven years old I told my parents I felt that I was ready to play, and we wondered if I was heavy enough to make the cut. My brothers had no problem weighing in when they were my age; however I was a different story. I was the skinniest and smallest for my age. I signed up to play on the Pop Warner C-Team.

Prior to the start of the season there was a league weigh-in for all teams. We were nervous because I had to weigh-in at least sixty-five pounds. So to play it safe my father put quarter rolls in my sweatpants pockets to help me make the cut. I stepped on the scale and when it registered sixty-one pounds I nearly passed out from disgust. Moments later the commissioner walked up to the scale after discussing something with my coach who was fortunately also my brother Michael. He looked into my eyes and must have seen the passion I had to play because he put his briefcase on the scale and sure enough the scale read sixty-five pounds. I let out a sigh of relief and my brother Michael winked at me.

I played a total of seven years of Pop Warner Football and five of them were on the C-Team. The C-Team was for the youngest and lightest players that were in the program. My father helped me dress for every one of my games. He ensured that every lace was tied and that I was the sharpest looking player out on the field. My first three seasons playing were completely awful: we didn't win a game and I was playing out of position. Can you imagine a four foot seven inches, sixty-one pounder playing tight end? I think I still have bumps and bruises from those years. My mother used to get so scared that I did not weigh enough and would feed me pasta and carbohydrates to help me pack on the pounds.

Things did get better due to a position change and practice. I started playing tailback, which had its ups and downs. One of the positive moments was when we won our first game against Danvers, which was the home of New York Giant great Mark Bavaro. There was thirty seconds left in the game, and we were trailing by five. I still remember the play like it was yesterday; it was a toss left and I put the jets on and ran fifty-two yards for a touchdown. I think my father ran with me the entire way, inspiring me with every step he took. To put the icing on the cake, Salem High legendary football Coach Ken Perrone was in attendance and witnessed the run and gave me the nickname Golden Boy.

Michael is a very enthusiastic coach who gets so upset when he loses that he fasts for a week. He coached me for the majority of my Pop Warner years and let me have it when I made bonehead mistakes. He was very intimidating and I used to fear him. Years later he explained to me why he was hard on me. He stated, "I am a perfectionist and I despise losing. I knew the potential that you had and wanted to get the most out of you and your teammates, you are my brother I wanted you to succeed even more, I could see the talent within you." For example when we were playing West Peabody and it was the end of the game we were driving down the field. It was fourth and goal, Mike called my number it was a toss right but I decided to get it and run away from my blocking and go left, which resulted in me getting gang tackled. I was quite aware I had messed up and knew that he was going to yell at me, so I decided to stay down and pretend I was hurt. I figured by doing this I would get some sort of sympathy, but boy was I wrong! The trainer was examining me and Mike came out on the field to see if I was all right. Once the trainer stated I was okay, Mike started doing his best intimation of Bill Parcells. He yelled so loud that I thought my helmet was going to crack. Sometimes his sidekick Doc Vaccaro would try to mellow him out but it seldom worked. My father still talks about that occurrence to this day.

Times were not always pleasant growing up. There was a specific period in my life that looking back at today and I am very fortunate to still be alive. I used to have a paper route throughout my neighborhood, Witchcraft Heights. Since I lived in a safe area I would complete the paper route after school by myself. The year was 1988, I was ten years old and I just started the fifth grade. I was halfway through my paper route when a silver car approached me and a man rolled down the window. The man asked me if he could buy one of my newspapers. I replied telling him that I only had enough newspapers for customers on my route and that I could not sell them individually. He would not take no for an answer and went on to tell me that he really needed the newspaper. He stated that all the local stores where sold out of them, and that he could pay me ten dollars for one newspaper. Since at that time the newspapers were only worth thirty-five cents I figured that it would be a quick nine dollars and some change. Therefore I decided to take him up on the offer and agreed to sell him one of my newspapers. I figured that I would just face the consequences later when I was a paper short. As I approached the driver's side window I extended my arm into the car to hand the guy the newspaper he took out the ten-dollar bill. As I reached for the money the man grabbed my arm and started to pull me into the car. Thank God that I was athletic and had on a lose jacket. I slipped out my jacket and ran into the closest house never looking back. That night a local policeman came by and we put together a sketch of the suspect.

A couple of weeks passed and my family and I started to receive death threats in the mail. These death threats were extremely violent and disturbing. That same week I got called down to the office in school and was told that my mother called. They said that she told them that we had a family emergency and that she was coming to pick me up. Therefore I got dismissed early and was told that she would pick me up behind the school. I made my way down to the location and noticed a similar silver car was parked there. Once I saw that silver car I turned around and ran back into the school.

By the time Halloween came it seemed like things blew over and I went trick or treating with a few of my friends. I dressed up as a pirate and did not have a worry in the world. Halloween in Witchcraft Heights is what children around American dream of, the streets are packed with families trick or treating and excitement fills the air. I had an excellent night and even got compliments from an older couple telling me that I won the scarcest costume contest. As a reward for the scarcest costume they took my picture and even gave me some extra candy.

The week after Halloween my family received another death threat in the mail, this time even more gruesome, it was devastating. The death threat stated that they were going to mutilate my mother and cut my head off. To make it even worse they had the picture of me that was taken on Halloween night. Hours later the city's detective arrived at my house and questioned my parents, brothers, Aunt and I. After the detective made some calls to get a search warrant, we took a ride over to the house where the mysterious photograph was taken. The house was only about a mile away from my house. I clung to my father in complete fright and my mother comforted me. I can still picture that scary old women staring into my eyes like a witch casting a spell on her victim. The couple was asked to locate the picture and they indicated that it was missing. The detective played the role of Sherlock Holmes and worked closely on the case.

Apparently my brother Eric who was a freshman in high school at the time was dating a senior in high school. Her ex-boyfriend could not digest this and wanted to retaliate. One of our neighbors whose father was the Salem Lieutenant and a couple of his friends put together this disturbing plot to retaliate. The grandmother of one of the kids was the lady who took my picture on Halloween. Justice was never served in this case and the main culprit that was involved is now a policeman in the City of Salem. This was an extremely disturbing time mentally in my life. Who knows what would have happened to me if I were ever caught by that man in the silver car. I thank God for my good judgment to slip my jacket off and run. If they got away with attempted kidnapping and death threats why couldn't they get away with murder. After this incident my parents wouldn't let me out of their sight.

The fall season of 1989 is when I came into my own as a football player playing on the C-Team. My brother Mike decided to coach the A-Team and left the C-Team duties to Howie Olson. Howie was a very creative coach who was designing plays in his sleep (and that's no exaggeration). He converted me to quarterback, which was a great move for me. However, I had over a hundred plays to learn. To help me, Howie used to type all the plays out and tape them inside my jersey. This was my breakout season. I did it all: running, passing, kicking and finishing the season by going 8–1. This was the most win's a C-Team has ever won in Salem Pop Warner history. There was a three-way tie for first place and the league decided to have a ten-yard fight, which would be the deciding tie-breaker. Our team won the coin toss and received a bye for the first round. When it was our time to play we were ready. We battled back and forth with Howie behind us with every trick up his sleeve. I scored four touchdowns, but it wasn't enough we lost by one score. Once again, we were denied the playoffs.

The following season we were a team to be reckoned with, going 9–0 and finally making the playoffs. We got beat up pretty bad but it was a great experience and I was starting to make a name for myself as a young rising star. Bruce Riccardi was my coach that year and really helped me improve my skills even though he was a little crazy. When it got dark out he would drive his car on the field and put on his headlights. His desire for the game made playing more fun and intense.

My final year of Pop Warner was very frustrating for me, but it was definitely a learning experience, which helped me get ready for my high school career. Our team did not do as well as the previous two seasons and it was hard on me losing. However this season was more physical, which helped me get ready for my high school football career. Mike coached me that season and he actually mellowed out a little, however this only lasted for just that season. My brother had us run the same plays in Pop Warner as they did in Salem high school. This helped me mentally; I was a step ahead of most of the other quarterbacks.

The hill of my football career was steep and long with many bumps in it. The sun was setting in the horizon, many walked this similar path and stumbled even fell. Some resurrected like Jesus while others drifted onto different paths. At a young age the dream was visible I could almost taste it. This is where my journey as a football player began. I was playing Pop Warner Football and was as focused as a child could be. Whistles blowing, parents watching, and the smell from the woods that surrounded the fields are the thoughts still with me when every August arrives. Not a worry in the world, playing a kids game is what laid the foundation for me to be able to live my dream. The stage was set for a story full of action, drama, suspense and a tone of glory that would far outweigh any pain.

5

CRUSADER OR WITCH

"It is in your moments of decision that your destiny is shaped."
—Anthony Robbins

Half way through my 8th grade school year, my father threw me a curve ball and told me he had registered me to take a placement test that would enable me to enroll at Bishop Fenwick High School. I was shocked because both of my brothers played football at Salem High. Salem also had a much more challenging athletic program than Bishop Fenwick did at the time. However Bishop Fenwick was a private school and had a better reputation for academics. It was then that my father explained that he was upset with the politics involved in the Salem High football program and how unhappy he was with the way my brother's were treated. I thought I was truly going to be a Bishop Fenwick Crusader. Yet after weighing the pros and cons, I decided to follow my brother's path and to become a Salem High Witch. The summer before my freshman year, my brother Mike was named Salem High freshman football coach. I was stunned, another year of intimidation, however I was excited he was going to coach me again.

My father and Mike were determined to see me have a successful career at Salem High. The same summer that Mike got hired my parents signed me up to attend the Northeast QB and Receiver Camp. This was a camp that was pivotal in my development and growth as a football player. Doug Wood and Jim Stehlin, the founders of the camp, are the best in the business. They were sticklers on good techniques and positive attitudes. This camp helped me get geared up for my high school football career.

My freshman football season my mother was concerned because of my size, which was only five foot six inches, one hundred and thirty pounds. Going into my freshman year my mother decided to up my food intake to help me put on some weight. However no matter how much food I ate my metabolism was so fast that it didn't help. Since there was no weigh-ins in high school football it was time to strap it up against some big boys. This didn't stop my mom from going to the games and cheering louder than the cheerleaders. That season we won the conference championship. I played very consistently and made a smooth transition from Pop Warner to high school football. My solid play contributed to me dressing for the varsity games, but I didn't see any action that season.

Freshman year basketball was extremely frustrating. My strongest asset as a basketball player was my ability to shoot. I played AAU/Junior Olympics growing up and I always had the green light to shoot during games. My team, Wildcat AAU, was playing Greater Boston, which had future Arkansas sharp shooter Pat Bradley. Pat and I shot the lights out of the ball, meaning we didn't miss a shot. I remember hitting fourteen three-pointers and laughing as I looked at my father's face and saw him sitting with his mouth open in disbelief. Both of us literally burned the nets off; by the end of the game both nets were ripped and hanging. My response was "Bring on Larry Bird." This is one of those things you had to be there to believe it. This is one of my favorite basketball memories. My freshman year was a difficult time period for me. The coach had a different philosophy of basketball than I had been accustom to, or ever heard of. His philosophy was if you attempted a three point shot you would be benched. The first game of the season I made a wide-open three-pointer and instantly got benched. Without saying the rest of the season was not fun.

Things turned out better in the spring with baseball. Charlie Felton was the freshman baseball coach and is a great person. I batted over .350 and played centerfield. That was the last year I really enjoyed playing baseball. For some reason baseball could not fill the same desire that I had for football.

The summer after my freshman year I started the strength shoes. They are designed to increase speed and power, and lifted weights, trying to crack one hundred thirty pounds. I also started to train with one of my brother Eric's good friends, Chris Carroll. He was a freshman at Sacred Heart College. He was encouraging and really helped me get ready for the upcoming season. By training with Chris he helped instill confidence in me. At this time one of my brother's close friends Chris Corneau asked me why I was working so hard, and if I wanted to play professionally someday. At that point in my career I realized that I could be a professional athlete someday and longed to be one. From that day on I did everything I could to make it to the next level.

The end of the summer of 1993 will forever be a sad time for my brother Eric and me. Jody Ryan who was Eric's best friend and a close friend of mine died tragically in a car crash. Jody was a very special person who taught me a lot about life. He was on his own since he seventeen and was working two jobs and putting himself through college. He brought a smile to everyone's face. He was always positive even though he was dealt with some very bad hands. I am very grateful I got to know someone as special as he was. Out of love and respect, three years later I got a tattoo around my arm in his honor

Through my sophomore football season I saw varsity time just as a place kicker. I remember kicking my first PAT and feeling like it was the kick to win the Super Bowl, I was pretty nervous. One moment that will stick in my mind forever was the game against Winthrop. If we won that game it would put us in the Super Bowl. There were fifteen seconds left and Coach Perrone decided to go for a field goal, if this attempt was made it would of won the game. I was ready but he called out Tony Cooper a player that had never kicked in a game. The week before that game, he joked around in practice and kicked during a special teams period, impressing the coaches. Tony ended up attempting the field goal and kicked the top of the ball and hit the long snapper in the ass. I was disgusted and started to wonder if that program was for me? My father set up a meeting with Bishop Fenwick officials about leaving Salem High and enrolling at Fenwick. Between us we decided to put it off until after the basketball season.

Defense is something I enjoyed playing when it came to basketball. If you could play defense then you would have enjoyed playing for coach Wayne Hanscom. He was the junior varsity coach and was very defensive orientated. That season was a very positive experience. I had a very solid season, which helped me move up to varsity by the end of the season. My first varsity shot attempt was successful. I remember walking into my house after the game and reading a sign my dad made that said "Congratulations 998 points to go."

My father grew up watching his high school basketball team dominate and win numerous Tech Tourney championships, which gave them the reputation of being one of the top teams in New England. With the cards my father was dealt in life he never got the opportunity to play. However he loved the sport and was delighted I shared the same desire. Both my brothers were strictly football players. My father said that, "Coming from a city like Somerville where basketball was such a high profile sport I felt quite proud that my son was able to compete for a high school team within a city that had a very successful past."

Rumors were being spread in the spring of my sophomore year that I would never start as quarterback for Salem, and once again my father was feeling that I would be another victim of politics in the Salem High system. It was evident by the statements I was hearing. After gym class one day one of the physical education teachers, harassed me by making similar statements that I would never be quarterback. I tried to ignore him but it bothered me because this guy did not know anything about me: my character, drive, and work ethic. Coach Perrone heard the news about what was going on and immediately set up a sit down with my father. The question was would Coach Perrone lie to my father's face? This made me wonder if I was going to play my final two seasons of football at Salem High?

This problem was secondary to an event that surfaced at the end of my sophomore school year that nearly changed my life forever. That May I attended the Salem High Senior Prom. During the post prom hours there was a small get-together at a motel. I was hanging out when all of sudden four African-American men roughly in their early twenties barged in our room. Apparently the door was unlocked. They looked around and started staring at me. At this point, I knew I was in trouble. They asked me to go outside because they wanted to talk and I agreed. At the last second, I made a dash for the bathroom. I looked for a window there was none and I tried to lock the door but it was broken. Seconds later they ran into the bathroom and said, "Why you running white boy?" and pulled out a gun. They went into my pockets and took the money I had as well as my beeper. Then they told me to turn around and put the gun to my head. They took off moments later and were never caught. I later found out they were a gang from Philadelphia that had ties to the Boston area. To this day I often think about what can happen when you are at the wrong place at the wrong time.

I started working at Forest River Park that summer, a historic park in Salem. Pioneer Village is a place, where pilgrims settled when they came over from England. The park has a public pool and I was doing pool maintenance with a lot of college kids who were friends with my brother, Eric. One night a week I would work pool security with my buddy Justin Kingston. The pool was located in a very secluded area in the park and to get out of the park you had to walk through half a mile of wooded area. One night when I was working pool security we got a call from our boss Zach Zegarowski at about 12:30A.M. He said we could leave and that he was running late, so to lock up and leave. As we made our way onto the trail that took us out of the park we heard some sticks break and Justin said, "Sean I think I saw something." I didn't think much of it. Ten more yards up the trail, I saw a shadow move behind a tree and then jump out in front of Justin. It looked like a very large man with a dark complexion decided to do my best imitation of Carl Lewis and ran as fast as I could, yelling for help. I ran about three hundred yards out of the park and into someone's backyard before a man came out of his house with a baseball bat and I told him about the incident. Justin caught up eventually out of breath and looked ghost white. We all walked to the parking lot and the Good Samaritan made sure we were all right and left. We sat in the car and locked the doors and just gave each other a look that indicated complete fright. The next thing we knew a large guerrilla jumped on the hood and started shaking the car. I tried starting the car and it wouldn't start. I thought I was watching an HBO horror video. I starting beeping the horn and finally the car started.

The guerrilla spotted our boss, Zack and started running after him. We decided to go to a pay phone and call the cops. As we drove out of the park we saw a crowd of people walking down a hill overlooking the park laughing hysterically. To top the prank off, Joe Curella, an employee at the pool was taking off the guerrilla costume. Boy we never lived that down! Yet again I related this episode to football as it was just another speed workout that was getting me ready for a season that I would not have expected in my wildest dreams.

6

FLYING WITCHES

✦

WITCH HUNT

"Adversity cause some men to break; others to break records."
—William A. Ward

The spring of my sophomore year I decided to have a talk with the head varsity football Coach, Ken Perrone. It was then that I told him I felt that if I were the starting quarterback I could help take our team to the Super Bowl. Lets just say that he thought I was on drugs. I was an inexperienced tiny sophomore, and only one Salem team had been to the Super Bowl in the ninety-five years of its existence, and that was twenty years ago. Little did he know that I would live up to everything that I promised!

The summer going into my junior year is when I decided it was time to train like one of the athletes I idolized growing up, Walter Payton. My theory was if you want to be the best you have to train like the best, and Payton truly was the best. I used the strength shoes religiously, which helped me with my speed and power. For the first time I really hit the weights, which contributed, to the development of my body. In addition, I threw about two to three hundred balls a day to one of my receivers AJ Grimes. I played competitive sports from an early age but I never had to compete for playing time until my junior year of high school. My junior year was the focal point in my athletic career and made me look at the game from a different perspective. When I practiced during the summer I used to visualize the moment, I'd throw the game winning touchdown pass to put our team in the Super Bowl, with the music from *The Natural* playing in my head. I truly believed that this vision would become a reality if I got the chance. However my only question was would I get the opportunity?

The controversy with the quarterbacks was really bad and got seriously out of control. Before the first game of the season my tires were slashed in the school parking lot. Fortunately a janitor witnessed the entire ordeal and it was linked to one of the quarterback's sisters that I was competing against. Everyone at school compared this to the Harding/Kerrigan incident that happened during the same time period. Also one of the contenders for the quarterback's spot was the eighth son of his family to play for the coach, this was hard to compete against. Even through all this distraction I stayed focused and had my goals set. Nothing was going to deter me from my promise I made to the coach; I was going to lead the team to the Super Bowl.

My hard work was noticed and paid off. I started in the first game of my junior season. We played the Peabody Tanners who were the number two team ranked in the state. They were a very talented team that made it to the Division I Super Bowl that season. I rotated with two other quarterbacks' and didn't attempt one pass or rush and watched the other two combine for five turnovers. We lost thirteen to nothing, and I was so upset after the game that I walked home from the field with my pads on. The field was not even close to my house and it was a good walk, I can only imagine what the people driving by me thought. I did a great deal of thinking that night and came to the conclusion I would continue to work hard and leave the rest up to the coaches. The following game I started again and on the first drive I threw my first varsity touchdown pass. Later in the game, I kicked the game winning field goal. During the next five games I only attempted eight passes, but I was starting and we were winning, so I was content.

The majority of Americans today think of the Witch Trials and hysteria when they think of Salem, Massachusetts. However seldom know the true meaning of the word "Salem" in Jerusalem means peace. The year 1692 in Salem, Massachusetts was a period where people were hunted down and falsely accused of practicing Witchcraft. These so called witches were hung and one eighty-one year old man was pressed to death. Nineteen men and women were hung during this time period. (*The Salem Witch Trials, Laura Marvel*). Who would have thought over three hundred years later in 1994 similar tactics would be used to oust the city's legendary football coach Ken Perrone who was a prime victim of a modern day Witch Hunt. Perrone achieved third place in Massachusetts for wins with a 256–84–11 record and was in his twenty-second season at Salem.

After we beat Lynn English on a Friday night our coaches informed us that the Salem teachers union was going on strike for the following Monday. Since the majority of the coaches were teachers in the Salem school system they were in a very tough predicament, especially since we were scheduled to play Swampscott the following week. The winner of that game would be in the driver's seat to go to the Super Bowl. If the coaches were to cross the picket lines and coach, it would put their jobs in jeopardy after the season.

Coach Perrone and the schools administration had tension between them. The administration sent a memo advising Coach Perrone and his assistant coaches to cease and desist from any and all athletic practices with the Salem High School Football team until they returned to their teaching assignment. Our team was caught in the throes of a teacher's strike that threatened to steal away our coach. Coach Perrone was feeling the effects of one of the strangest weeks in high school football history. The saga attracted intense media attention and distracted us from a most important week of preparation. When our team took the field for practice the following week, it looked like we were the New England Patriots. All the major news channels and newspapers were interviewing players and coaches. It was a very emotional time that really upset a lot of the members of our football family.

There were a lot of distractions that week but the coaches did a great job of keeping us focused. The Salem teacher strike affected four thousand eight hundred school children and five hundred and six schoolteachers. They were on strike for a total of ten days (*Salem Evening News, Nov. 1994*). I got the general impression that the administration was mainly concerned with the budget. I remember reading the Boston Globe sports the day before the game and the editor predicted us to lose 40–10 and stated: "Too many distractions." I cut it out and used it for bulletin board material to motivate our team. I don't think Swampscott knew that in the off-season I used to workout on their field. This was like a home game for me; I felt that I too had the home field advantage.

Even after all this time and all my football experience, that Swampscott game is one of my fondest memories as an athlete. We played the Swampscott game in front of well over ten thousand people in early November and it was over seventy degrees. I had what the coaches called my breakout game. Throwing two touchdowns passes and kicking a field goal, thanks to our excellent line giving me time to throw. Our defense held Swampscott's high-powered offense to well below their average and we won 16–8. I received player of the game honors and was interviewed on Sports Channel after the game. Perrone, who defied the administrations order not to coach in the game, called the victory over Swampscott the most "fulfilling and satisfying" in his thirty-seven years as a coach. In athletic terms I was in the zone. This is when you take your abilities to another level and all the drama occurring before you becomes secondary. I never was on a team before where players just refused to lose. We were fifteen to eighteen year old kids receiving just as much media hype as the Patriots and handling the adversity like we were veterans to these types of situations. The transition we made was just remarkable.

Believe it or not the administrators had the audacity to try to dissolve our football team. Everything that education stands for suddenly became questionable in our minds when the administrators turned their backs on us. We felt abandoned. Our coaches defined what a educator stood for while the administrators tried to have incompetent people take over the team during the strike. This was only shortchanging the kids who were trying to live out there dream, by making it to the Super Bowl. A portion of our team came from single parent families and the coaches were like father figures instilling values that were never known to them before. Unity, hard work, passion and believing in yourself is what the 1994 Salem High team stood for and that bond was too strong for some small-city political group to break. Coach Perrone's thoughts on the teachers strike: "I wish the strike never happened but I feel the coaches did the right thing honoring the teachers by participating in the strike. The coaches got the blessing of the teachers to cross the picket line and coach. If the strike happened again tomorrow we would do the same thing. We knew the school days could be made up but these kids might not be able to play for a championship again."

The following week we played at Winthrop. Winthrop is the home of Mike Enrizone, who scored the game-winning goal in hockey against Russia in the 1980 Winter Olympics. He just happened to be at the game. I think he sprinkled some of his magic on Miller field. The game against Winthrop was later titled, "Do you believe in miracles?" A pre-game ritual is something athletes do before sporting events to help them prepare mentally before they perform. I started pre-game rituals in the 8th grade. I would watch the *Why the Eagles Soar*, which was basically a Doug Flutie highlight film. One specific play that is known as the 'Pass' that is against Miami, which beat them with no time left and basically won Flutie the Heisman Trophy. That play stuck with me ever since the first time I witnessed it. It was basically a miracle. Our game against Winthrop was a game very similar to Flutie's game versus Miami. There was four seconds left and we were trailing by seven. We were on their forty five-yard line and I threw a bullseye to Many DePena who caught the ball in full stride at the back of the end zone. The two-point conversion was good by the E-Train and we won with no time left on the clock. There was another miracle in Winthrop but this time it wasn't pertaining to Hockey. As an athlete you dream of finding yourself in these situations, and I had this opportunity at a young age and was overwhelmed. A lot of critics say you need luck, but all "luck is when preparation meets opportunity." The headlines in the paper the next day read *Stellato Works Flutie Magic.* I thought that it was cool to be associated with Flutie. This pass was also televised nationwide on channel seven as one of the top seven sporting events that occurred that past week nationwide, which was titled *Seven wonders of the week.* I placed number six just behind Drew Bledsoe, who at the time was the starting quarterback for the New England Patriots.

We still had one team standing in our way Beverly, our archrival that we played on Thanksgiving Day. Beverly was 8–1 and very solid. That weather was very cold but it didn't stop over fifteen thousand fans from attending. We battled the entire game and with one minute remaining we were leading 10–7. It was fourth down and one yard to go and they had the ball on their own thirty six-yard line. The play that the Beverly coached called was a running play up the middle from the sidelines all you saw was twenty-two players go into a pile and their running back coming out of it. When it looked like the play was over, he scooted sixty six-yards for a touchdown. Let's just say that Beverly thought that they were going to the Super Bowl, I guess they had already forgotten what we pulled off at the Winthrop game with only four seconds left. I'm not going to lie, my stomach turned but with fifty three seconds on the clock, I knew they left too much time, and now it was time for me to do my best impression of Joe Montana. We got the ball on our own 35-yard line and failed to convert until fourth down, when Beverly got called for pass interference. That moved the ball to midfield. The next three plays we got stuffed, and on 4th down our old reliable line gave me some time. I found Manny DePena running a skinny post and he made it down to their three yard line. Two plays later our running back, Elvin Rodriguez, (The E-Train) scored, and I lived up to my promise: we were going to the Super Bowl. Little did I know at the time, that my future wife was watching me from the opponent's side of the stands. The following week we received a ton of national publicity and lost the Super Bowl. I was heartbroken from the loss but I will cherish that year for the rest of my life. It was a wonderful experience to be able to play for Coach Perrone. He is one of the most genuine coaches that I have ever played for.

That same school year, we went 25–0 and won the state championship in basketball. I finally got what all athletes strive for, a championship ring. To put the icing on the cake we were the last high school team to play at the legendary Boston Garden. I got goose bumps when I stepped on the court that night and thought back to those many nights when my father used to tell me stories about how those sixteen NBA Championships were won. That night was a very special night for my father and myself. He basically grew up in that building and to see me play on the same floor as the legends was a real touching experience for the both of us.

7

OWA GUIDANCE FROM ABOVE

◆

TURNOVER

"You take a setback and turn it into a come back."
—Anonymous

Owa was the nickname my oldest brother Michael gave to my grandmother when he was little because he could not pronounce Grandma. Inspiration touches people's lives in many different ways. For me, it will always be my grandmother who was my father's mother, she passed away at the end of my junior year of high school at our home in Salem.

Lillian Stellato was everything a grandmother should be. She gave me unconditional love even when I was an immature adolescent and closed-minded. She passed away when I was seventeen and before I was mature enough to tell her everything she meant to me. Owa and I had our arguments over silly stuff but no grudges were ever held. I usually triggered the argument due to the fact I was very cognitive dissonance and only saw certain issues from my point of view. It saddens me that I never had the chance to tell her the impact and inspiration she had on my life. She was very spiritual and I know she is smiling at me from above because of the type of person I have become and the commitment I have made to God.

My other grandmother was Shirley Destefano. She passed away when I was only three years old, therefore I do not really have any vivid memories of her.

However my grandmother's memories live strong through my mother and I have come to know the person she was. I am blessed to have my mother share her cherished memories of my grandmother. The values my grandmother instilled in my mother were carried down to me. I pray that some day I can keep her spirit alive and carry the same values down to my children. I am forever grateful to have such remarkable women as my mother and grandmothers in my life.

Owa lived with my other grandmother Shirley for fifteen years in an apartment in Revere until Shirley passed away. Then she moved in with my family where she lived her last fourteen years of her precious life. She was a strong and proud Italian woman who never stopped working. She never wanted anyone's help to make ends meet and she always had a way in doing so. She taught me that things would not just be handed to you in life and that there is no substitution for hard work. She retired from working for Filenes in Boston at eighty-five years old and she used to make the commute by bus five days a week. I can't even imagine making that commute via public transportation; this simply amazes me that she did that. When I was younger I didn't realize how demanding that must have been for her. She was also a widow for over thirty-eight years. She had worked her entire life.

Growing up on Sunday afternoon after those hard-hitting Pop Warner games my Owa would start preparing her homemade pasta and sauce. My mother would always be in the kitchen helping her cook. Owa's Sunday pasta was a treasured Stellato family ritual. A better ritual was Christmas Eve. She used to prepare the seven fishes, which is a religious Italian tradition. She stuffed calamari, which is cooked squid; stuffed lobsters were just a couple of her mouthwatering dishes. My father, both of my brothers and I used to play catch on the street and we could smell the food from outside. I have always loved lobster so I would always make sure that I got the seat next to her because she would always give me part of her lobster tail without anyone noticing.

She was one of the most generous people I ever met. If one of her loved ones wanted something, even if she was down to her last dollar, she would buy it for them.

Owa supported my brothers and me in everything we did. Although she never attended any of my games because of her physical condition, I know her prayers were often answered.

Growing up, I was fascinated by Sherlock Homes and wanted to be a detective. So every Sunday night Owa would make popcorn, and we would watch *Murder She Wrote*. I would always try to solve the crime, sitting there with a notebook and a corn pipe to try to outsmart Jessica Fletcher. Each time I figured something out; she would give me a quarter. If I solved the murder she would give me a dollar. When my parents would go out for the night my Grandma would watch us, and we would raise hell unless she would tell us stories about Italy. She used to talk about the old country: its beauty and unique traditions.

During Thanksgiving 1991, Owa was diagnosed with a heart condition that required possible surgery on her valves. Owa did not want to go through with the procedure because she did not feel she was strong enough to survive the operation. She stayed upbeat through it all and continued to work until she retired the following May.

My junior football season I went through a lot mentally. I dealt with politics in Salem High football, people vandalizing my property and challenges of demanding academic classes. People were constantly trying to tell me what I could not do. Owa was there through thick and thin and stayed very supportive. She listened to all the games on the radio and got such a thrill seeing me do something special that my two older brothers were never given the chance to do, win a championship in dramatic fashion. The Thanksgiving of 1994, Owa fell at home, which contributed to her failing health. In fact, at my 17th birthday party Owa started crying as soon as my Mom lit the candles and said that this would be her last birthday with me. That hit me hard and I started crying as we hugged each other. Each year on my birthday I have flashbacks to that very moment.

For as long as I live, April 30, 1995 is a night that will stay with me. My parents were out and Owa called me to come downstairs; she sat me down and held my hand and started talking. Prior to that day we never had a close Grandma to grandson talk. She indicated how proud she was of me and told me to continue to work hard because good things would materialize. Then she looked me in the eyes and said "Grandma is going to die." I completely collapsed in her lap and started weeping. This is the first time I ever revealed that story to anyone. Two days later on May 2, 1995, Lillian Owa Stellato passed away at 88 years old. I came home from school and saw a few cars in front of our house and didn't think anything of it. But when I walked into the living room and saw Michael with his hands on his head, crying, I just collapsed. My first reaction was just a sense of bitterness. I just couldn't understand why this had happened now. As time passed I became relieved that her suffering was over, that she had gone to heaven to be reunited with her soul mate Pasquale. My grandmother instilled strength into me that I have been able to utilize ever since she has passed away.

Owa's dying brought my father and I even closer. That was the first time I ever witnessed him crying and it hurt me. From that day on, I promised myself I would never say or do anything to hurt him. This may be difficult at times however we both know the love and bond we have with each other. We also came to the realization that it is okay to disagree. I am blessed to have such a wonderful man in my life.

When I'm alone with my thoughts, I often think about my grandmother's life and the sacrifices she made for her family. I think about the inner strength and the faith she displayed right up until her last days on earth. When I'm having a bad day and things are not materializing as planned I say: *Sean, if Owa could live widowed for 38 years and fight off a serious heart problem for as long as she did, what obstacle is ever going to be in my life that I cannot conquer?*

For this reason, I write "Owa" with a permanent black marker on the inside of my left forearm, with an arrow pointing towards heaven before each game I play. Anytime I felt fatigued I looked at my forearm and thought 'I'm tired?...no, I'm doing what I love to do and have the most supportive and caring family in the world.' I looked to this marking for inspiration. It gives me strength from within when I need it the most. This is the type of strength you really never know you have until you really concentrate and try to utilize your thoughts the right way.

I was blessed with supportive parents, health and strength as a child. The sports I choose and longed to play were always a challenge for me because of my size. I was labeled at a young age and was told I would not be able to succeed in the athletic avenues I wanted to pursue. Because of my family and my Owa I was able to achieve and go after my dreams. To this day my Owa is my inspiration. Scouts and the experts put too much emphasis on size and forty-yard dash speed. Certain players are just blessed faster, Who does not even have to work on their skills. I have had tons of people say to me, "Aren't you too small to play pro-football? You're only 5'9." I ask them, " Have you ever put the pads on and truly know what the game is all about? Size doesn't have anything to do with it; you can't measure someone's heart." This vital ingredient, heart along with my inspiration will lead me through the toughest times.

Keeping Owa's memory with me at all times will continue to drive me forward as a person giving me the constant energy I need. That is why, starting in my junior college football season I began to leave Owa a ticket for every game I played in and I haven't stopped that practice to this day. I believe she is one of my guardian angels and inspiration. In January 2003, I got a tattoo of a cross on my left shoulder in Owa's memory. I know she will always be with me. Something as little as a remembrance written in ink could play a significant role in getting an edge over your opponent and finish the task at hand.

8

THE GUNNERY FIRST &
LONG

**"Ask and you will receive seek and you will find; knock, and it
will be opened to you."**

—Matthew 7:7

Prior to my senior year at Salem High School I should have transferred, it was a complete nightmare. After my senior football season I did not receive any scholarship offers from Division I schools. I attribute this to the fact that Coach Perrone and his staff got fired. The start of my senior football season the team was loaded and was chosen by the coaches in the preseason poll to win the league. However, the first two games we played tough and lost. This is when people started pointing fingers and players started to drop off the team. The starting running back that helped lead us to the Super Bowl the previous year quit the team after the second game because of racial slurs from the coaching staff. By season's end, fourteen players quit. I went from as high on life as a seventeen year old could be, to a low depression by end of my senior football season.

One day after practice Warren Armes who was the head football coach took me aside in a corner and starts talking all sort of non-sense. He said that he heard that I had been talking to Coach Perrone and if he were running the show we would be going to the Super Bowl. He told me this was bullshit and to suck his dick and grabbed my neck. I was completely shocked and knew the rest of the year would be hell. I did not go to the administration because I was in fear that the coach would state that I made this up and then not start me nor play me. Some how I kept my vision clear and my dream in mind and remained throughout the season. It was a rough season however I managed to break a handful of records along the way and got some new highlights for prep school.

I was the only senior to go on to play football the following year. This was because of the initiative my father and I took to contact teams and send out tape. Deep down I knew I could play Division I football and only wanted to play Division I, so I decided to go the prep school route. It came down to a real big school called Northfield Mount Herman or The Gunnery, a small prestigious school nearly three hours away. We choose The Gunnery because they gave me a very attractive financial package for a postgraduate year.

The transition from Salem High to Gunnery Prep was like night and day. Mostly because I was used to my wonderful home life, which consisted of my mother's great cooking. Living three hours away from home, with no television, refrigerator or radio in my room, and using phone conversations to try to make up for physical proximity with my loved ones, I had a hard time adjusting. I was used to sleeping in on the weekends. School on Saturdays, thousand word papers weekly, 6:00 A.M. wake ups daily were difficult to get used to. Coming out of Salem High I was not the most diligent student and I really struggled on the SAT's, scoring only an eight hundred. During my time at The Gunnery I was pushed to the limit both physically and mentally. I was willing to sacrifice things that I was very accustomed to in my everyday living. I had little choice. I wanted to succeed.

The Gunnery is located in Washington, Connecticut, which is about a three-hour car ride from Salem, Massachusetts. Route 47 is off interstate 84 and it is in the middle of nowhere. It was about fifteen miles from stores or the movie theater and was located on the hill. As we drove up the steep hill that was like a mountain I nicknamed the school "Gunnertraz" because it was isolated like Alcatraz. At this point I started to get emotional and my mother tried to soothe me, saying, "Don't worry, by the time you leave here, they are going to remember the name 'Stellato!'"

The head football coach, Hugh Caldara, made me feel very comfortable and was like my father away from home. He basically gave me the football and told me, "Just put points on the board and show this community the caliber of player we got." Those words instilled a great deal of confidence in me. Our first game at Suffield Academy was a frustrating experience. I was seeing my parents for the first time in a month and was ready to start a new chapter in my life. Our team got beat up pretty badly that day. It was towards the end of the game and I was hurting physically when my father came down to the sidelines to check on me. Well I lost it and went nuts, yelling at him, saying I didn't want to go to this school in the first place, and he was selfish for sending me there, and I was leaving. That night I did some soul searching and came to the conclusion that this place would benefit me the most in the long run and I decided to stick it out.

The following week things got tougher from an academic standpoint. At Salem, I wrote one book report in four years and now I was getting one thousand word papers weekly and a three-hour study hall period each evening. There was seldom any "Sean time." I kept on telling myself "When the going gets tough, Stellato's get going." The next football game was a lot different than the first one. My parents and brother made the trip to the game. I ended up having a great game scoring two touchdowns and one was a punt return. We won the game, which put the icing on the cake. I received headlines the next day in the Hartford Current, which is one of the most well known printed-papers in Connecticut.

I spent many of my evenings that fall exploring the philosophy of Jack Kerouac's *On the Road*, Shakespeare's *MacBeth* and *Dracula*. In addition, I was polishing up my role in a production of Shakespeare's *The Tempest*. Having a tough academic schedule helped me to excel in athletics at The Gunnery because I had no extra time to mess up. I credit my experiences at The Gunnery for expanding my horizons. The co-educational school had only two hundred thirty five students in the entire school and an average class size of twelve to fifteen students. This was a big adjustment for me, classes at Salem were about thirty students and my graduating class was about three hundred plus. At The Gunnery whenever I had trouble in a subject I would stop by my teacher's house at night. That was very easy to do, since most of my teachers lived right on campus.

The Gunnery is where I learned the value of time management. This very distinguished school pushed me on all cylinders to strive for perfection. Three-hour study halls a night were very vital for me. I missed this valuable element of study hall in high school, which helped make my transition into college much easier. The factor that ultimately had more of an effect on my future was my SAT scores. I raised them from 800 to 1100 and generated some interest from a couple of ivy-league schools. My parents were very proud. It made me really appreciate the work of Shakespeare and Jack Kerouac. I got to interact with people from different countries and ethnic backgrounds. I guess having very little "Sean time" was good because I was always busy and this made it easier for me not to get homesick or in trouble.

The challenge I faced academically made me study like a determined and focused student realizing football could only take me so far. I looked at the 1,000 word papers we had weekly and the Saturday classes as challenges that would test my character. I remember Friday nights before games in Salem I'd be out with my buddies or watching football films to force me to think about the game the next day. At The Gunnery, I would be in a small room that consisted of a bed, desk, and alarm clock reading *On the Road*, using the glare from the moon as my light because lights out would cut into my reading time. This would put me in a relaxing state of mind that helped me visualize the game and helped me understand the notion that it was only a game.

But when it was time to turn my emotion towards football, I made out just fine. Calling to mind the suffering I had endured through a trying senior year at Salem High, going 2–6–2 and adapting to the fallout of long time Coach Ken Perrone's ouster, I used this as fuel to the fire. I met every expectation as a football player at The Gunnery. Being named to First-Team All New England in the prep school ranks, while rushing for more than one thousand yards and accounting for nearly two thousand yards of total offense as a quarterback. Our team finished 3–5, which could have easily been 7–1 but that is the game of football, a game of inches.

It was a couple of days before we were playing one of our rivals, Canterberry Prep, which was a very good team that was undefeated. It was a school tradition to have an all sport bon fire, which was like a pep rally to boost school morale. Well that night about 15 starters decided to get crazy and make a dummy with a shirt on it that said "f*ck crew," pertaining to our crew team. Apparently the football team and crew team had a conflict. The next day Coach Caldara addressed the team and suspended the 15 starters. I was shocked we were lacking team depth and had to play one of the top teams in prep school football. It was basically our junior varsity team and me who were suited up the next day. After the first quarter, we were losing 17–0 and looking like the Bad News Bears, when all of sudden it was like a magic wand hit us. I fired the offensive line up and they started giving me enough time to make plays. I threw a touchdown pass and ran in a two-point conversion and we got some momentum. Our defense forced a turnover, and we drove the field and I scored on a bootleg right before the half to make it 17–14. Although we lost the game I was very happy to be a member of that team. We were totally outmatched but we managed to give one of the top teams in New England a good scare. At the end of the season I was selected the team's Most Valuable Player which was a nice accomplishment and I was pleased to be recognized by the team for my efforts. But the big question on my mind was where I would go to college?

I still had some unmet expectations as a basketball player that I wanted to fulfill. I knew it was going to be tough due to the fact that they had only won two games in the last two seasons. Our coach, John Russillo was a high tempered pizone (friend) that got his point across very clearly. That season we won a lot more games than the year before, and I finally started to have fun again while playing basketball, something I was a stranger to due to the politics that surrounded the Salem High program. I had two games where I scored over forty points and scored double digits every game, by season's end I was averaging 21 points, 8 assists and 3 steals per game. But would that be enough to get me into the All-New England Prep All-Star game? This would consist of twenty-four players from six states. Coach Russillo didn't hear anything the day when all the coaches were supposed to be informed if their players were selected. I'm not going to lie, that night when they called "lights out" I was really upset because I felt I always got sort of short changed as a basketball player and felt I could play with the best of them. Next thing I knew, someone was pounding my door down and I jumped up thinking I was in trouble. It was Coach Russillo with a memo stating I was chosen to play in the All-Star game. He gave me a big hug and said "Get your butt back into bed before we both get in trouble." The game itself was a confidence booster and I held my own against some future Division I players. That is when I realized I wanted to and could play Division I college basketball. At the team banquet, I was selected team M.V.P.

Every term at The Gunnery I made the honor roll. I applied and got recruited by 13 schools. I went to the Columbia vs. Cornell game and fell in love with Columbia. I met current San Diego charger Marcellius Wiley. Due to my low SAT II scores I didn't get into Columbia. So it came down to Richmond or a school I never heard of before, Marist College. I fell in love with Richmond and received a partial athletic scholarship but Marist came back with more money and it was closer to home. I didn't mind the distance but I knew it would be more realistic for my parents to come see me play if I chose Marist, not to mention having the opportunity to play Division I basketball. I picked Marist, which was a Division I-AA program located in Poughkeepsie, New York. I looked at this like, no matter whatever happened with my college selection at that point I knew that I was much better off than I was before I had attended that exclusive prep school tucked away in the wooded hills of Washington, Conn. While attending The Gunnery I grew out of my adolescence and turned into a young man with great expectations.

Since I had always been the runt of my family it was hard for me to put on weight. I was taller then my brother Michael, however it was a lot easier for him to gain muscle mass. In high school my brother Eric was a force to be reckoned with weighing in at 240 pounds with a fifty-four inch chest. While I was at The Gunnery I decided that if I wanted a chance to play Division I with the big boys then I would have to put on some weight. Therefore I went through extreme measures. I put on twenty-three pounds of muscle from February through May, which required a great deal of food consumption as well as a lot of weight training. Gratefully The Gunnery café staff was friendly and knew I was on a mission to put on weight. I went as far as eating a dozen egg whites a day and drinking almost a gallon of whole milk a day. My protein intake grew from one hundred grams a day to well over two hundred grams a day. At The Gunnery I did not have access to a refrigerator and once the cold weather came I used to hang a pillowcase out the window and stored food in it, which would keep it from spoiling.

At the time The Gunnery weight room was getting remodeled. Therefore I got a key to an area of the school, which was a small building with neither heat nor electricity. If the room had electricity I would have needed supervision. It was filled with very rusty old machines and weights. The smell of mill-dew was strong and the draft could be felt but this is where I started to develop my body and ability to be able make it at the collegiate level. The only problem with these workouts was that they had to be done at 4:45A.M. in the pitch black, all by myself, with my vision and memories as my only inspiration. Once in a while the moon would light the room a little. Since the school was located in New England, I had to wear four layers of clothing to keep myself warm. I used to say to myself that if I can get motivated for these workouts with these conditions then I could make it to the next level and play in any kind of weather conditions with out it affecting my physical capability.

The Gunnery was a crucial year in my life; it helped me mature as a person and develop into a student-athlete. In addition it made me completely realize that the world had more to offer than just football. The Gunnery instilled a confidence in me that I had never known existed and taught me that I could really do anything if I put my heart and mind to it. One of my grand plans is to donate enough money someday to help build the school a football stadium.

Even in the toughest times we managed to smile
and stay upbeat: from left to right: Eric, Dad,
me, Mom and Michael.

Here I am all smiles, just loving life.

My Nana Shirley, my mom just staying
cool on a summer day.

The Stellato boys styling in the eighties, from
left to right: Eric, me, and Michael.

My true inspiration Owa and my beautiful
mother before my 8th grade graduation.

You can see who got all the size, my brother
Eric doing an impression of Lou Ferigno.

I was more of a passer than runner in high school. Here I show my abilities picking up a key first down during my breakout game against Swampscott.

Running in the open field for some of my many yards in the prestigious Agganis All-Star game.

Football media day at Marist College.

A good receiver finds the end zone.
This was one of the most exciting
touchdown runs I had in my career.

Running the point for the Marist Basketball team.

Here I am with my brothers and nephew Michael
From left to right: Eric, Michael, and me.

Pulling the speed sled with fierce determination.
It sums up my journey constantly fighting adversity
and resistance. This is where I let out my frustration
and found my true self.

I pride myself on my sculpture;
I worked so hard to develop it. Some of
my teammates in college nicknamed me
Atlas.

Senior day at Marist College.

I enjoy reaching out to the youth;
we both get something out of it. (Tim Porco)

Running a route against the Carolina Rhinos.
Many things were going though my head
that night playing in my first pro game was one
of them.

Inside the huddle during a television timeout.
As you can see we had some big boys. (Tim Porco)

A lot of things go through my mind
when I am getting ready to run a route. (Tim Porco)

Here I am with Mike Summers after a Louisville Fire game.

My three nephews with their game faces on:
From left to right: My Godson Troy, Godson Vincent and Michael Jr.

My boxer Sly that I brought home from Memphis
for my fiancé relaxing on the beach.

The true bond between a father and son, my father
and I vacationing in Bermuda.

My true love and soul mate Krista
and I enjoying a night out.

(Tim Porco)

9

MARIST COLLEGE RED FOXES SAFETY

"Dictionary is the place that success comes before work. Hard work is the price we must pay for success. I think you can accomplish anything if you're willing to pay the price."
—Vince Lombardi

I committed to Marist College on May 1, 1997, and boy would I get some unpleasant surprises. I still remember the day I arrived on campus. The captains held a meeting and told the entire freshman class that nobody cared about how they did in high school and that college was as different as night and day. Moments later, we had a position meeting and twelve quarterbacks got introduced; I could not believe my eyes. I just told myself to do what I had done my entire career: outwork my competition and prove the critics wrong. I received a partial athletic scholarship, which helped to an extent, but Marist is a pricey college.

I never lost sight of the fact that my main reason for attending Marist was to receive a quality education. I knew that a degree from Marist would make my stock rise in the corporate world. For me, the main reason why I knew I would leave Marist with a diploma was because of my parents' sacrifices. I was aware my father did not have a pension and it was costing them a great deal. Not to mention, they were spending more than double on my education than my eldest brother Michael's who went to Salem State College. Neither of my parents attended college and they were very proud of the fact that I was going not to mention playing a Division I sport.

My major was Communications/Public Relations with a minor in Business/ Human Resource Management. I always liked to present or speak on behalf of a group and I felt like a communications major would prep me for a professional team's PR job. I could not see myself stuck behind a desk doing the 8A.M. to 5 P.M. day. I had the notion I liked to talk a lot and felt comfortable doing it so why not try to make a career out of it. I had high expectations as a student due to the progress I made in the classroom at prep school. From a football position, I was coming off a stellar prep school season and was told I would get time as a freshman and the job would be mine to lose the following season. The question that lingered with me was would I even get the opportunity to play quarterback?

My first game of my freshman year was an experience I will never forget. We were playing at Army on a Friday night against the Army junior varsity team. The thought that I was playing a team that dropped me from their recruiting list was all the motivation I needed. The coaches told me that I would play the second half at quarterback. Watching the first half from the sidelines made my stomach turn. We were down 16–0 and had no offensive momentum. Coach Polumbo let us have it at half time. This was a special night because it was my parents wedding anniversary and the last twelve years playing football I scored a touchdown for them. On the first play, I went in and I ran the ball for about ten yards and got hit good, which got the adrenaline going. The next play, I dropped back to pass, got pressure, and took off. I picked up about thirty-five yards but hurt my ankle. The ironic thing about it was that no one hit me. I just turned it inwards on the turf. I started limping to the sideline to get the play but stopped, tightened my shoelaces, and said to myself: "Pain is temporary pride is forever." Two plays later, I scored on a ten-yard keeper and then rushed for a two-point conversion. I could barley get up and a lineman helped me off the field. I was excited but in the back of my mind I knew my ankle was really messed up. We lost the game but I was feeling good about my efforts. My parents were very concerned about my physical condition and decided to drive me back to campus instead of me taking the bus.

The following day was the next varsity game at Iona, and I made the travel list. I don't think I went to bed that night because I iced my ankle so much. The next morning I remember trying to put pressure on it and I was like an alarm clock for the entire dorm because of the scream I let out. I ended up limping to the bus. I taped the ankle tight and attempted to do pre-game warm-ups but there was no use. The injury sidelined me for four weeks and put me deeper on the depth charts. I suited up for the Fairfield game and felt good. Good enough to run for a seventy-yard touchdown and extra point with a bad wheel (ankle). We lost 10–7 but I felt I was making a smooth transition to college football.

I didn't play in any more football games that season. The lies I was fed only made me hungry to succeed. The coaches would tell you one thing and do the opposite. For example "You had a great week of practice and deserve to make the travel squad." A day later your name is not on the list.

An event during my freshman year of college almost caused one of my closest friends his life because there was a lack of communication and friends not taking him seriously. He was my roommate and teammate at Marist. He was suffering from depression. Breaking-up with his girlfriend, not getting playing time on the football field, demanding computer science major and alcohol helped this young man hit rock bottom. One night he just started making statements like "I can't take it anymore, it's not worth it, and its time to put it all to an end" and he barged out of the room. I could hear the fear in his voice and knew to take him seriously therefore I decided to follow him. As I followed him he said that the Hudson Bridge would do the job. As we walked through the campus and into the City of Poughkeepsie he went from yelling to crying. He was about six feet tall and two hundred and forty pounds so I knew with the rage it would be tough to keep him in one place. I decided to run into someone's house and called 911. As I caught up to him he must have had an idea of what I did and started running for the bridge. He was only yards away from the bridge when I decided to use my football instincts and tackled him as hard as I could. I completely stunned him and partially knocked him out. He looked up at me and we both started to get emotional. I think that he realized that he had a true friend and life has its twist and turns but it's not worth ending it. We got a police escort back to our dorm room. That night we stayed up all night and had a heart to heart talk. Today he is living his life to the fullest and has thanked me numerous times for that heroic event that saved his life.

The following week I didn't get any action in football so I decided to get ready for basketball workouts. This is when my schedule got very demanding. For a month straight, I would wake up at 5:00 A.M. tape my ankle, then jog two miles, go to the gym, work on all my drills until 7:30A.M., attend class from 8:00 A.M. until 12:30 P.M., eat lunch and get ready for football practice, eat dinner, and then go to study hall. The two days of basketball workouts are both days that will stick with me. "Persistence" and "Perseverance" are words that got me through those two intense days.

The first day I stepped on the court it was weird standing next to Tom Kenney who was 6'11," Tomaz Cielebak who was 6'10," a swingman from Poland who barely spoke English, sharp shooting transfer from Providence, Bo Larigan, Puerto Rican Olympian Bobby Jo Hatton, and Dick Vitale's pre-season diaper dandy, a player who I will respect forever, Drew Samuels. Then you have me a 5'9" white-boy sticking out like a sore thumb. The Head Coach Dave MaGarrity was a 6'8," 300-pound high tempered coach that got his point across very clearly. It was the second day of workouts and coach must have thought practice was going awful or maybe he thought it was time to test the mental toughness of his new recruits. There was a drill called 22's which was a conditioning drill, and the object was to put a player at the foul line to shoot a one and one. If the player misses, the entire team runs the length of the court four times and if one player doesn't do it in fewer than 22 seconds you run it again. The drill ends when every player hits two free throws. Well, it was like both hoops were straight out of a carnival setting, where it's nearly impossible to hit and all twelve players missed. Coach started putting barrels at the corners of the court, guys were throwing up and numerous Europeans players were letting out unknown slang phrases.

Finally coach called out my name and I walked to the line, one of the players, Joe "Jumping" MaCurdy, approached me and said, "Sean you realize if you hit these two free throws you're going to make the team and if you don't you might as well walk into the locker room." I just looked at him and said to myself that he doesn't know that I'm like Joe Montana when it comes to pressure and got into the "Stellato Zone." Seconds later I sank both free throws and basically got carried off the court. Coach revealed to me later in the locker room that I would be wearing number twenty-five. That season was a very exciting experience. I only got to play in two games but I did do some traveling. I actually flew on an airplane for the first time to California to play Pepperdine. I stayed in my seat for six straight hours and sweated through my dress shirt.

Marist College basketball was a dream come true. All the hype that is made about playing Division I became a reality. From drugs, girls, athletes not doing their school work, to players receiving extra benefits just like how it is portrayed in the movies is what I witnessed first hand. I was the fourth player from Salem High School to make it to an illustrious Division I program. Rick Brunson, Scoonie Penn and Jamal Camah all accomplished this task. Playing as basketball players at Marist College was amazing; we were like the celebrities of the campus. Because of this the basketball team never bonded with the football team well, this was simply because of the way we got treated on the basketball team. The basketball team flew first class as well as stayed at five star hotels. Even though we were treated first class lets just say some players didn't act top shelf. I will always remember one player after team dinners on the road who would discretely take the tip and make the remark that "Mothers Day was coming." I remember going into the locker room before my first college basketball game and into my locker. I felt like a child on Christmas day, my locker was stacked with brand new Reebok sneakers, socks, wrist bands, sweat suits and warm ups dry cleaned and ironed. The jersey even had my name on the back of it.

After the basketball season, I still had pain in my ankle and got an MRI, which would indicate if there was any damage in the tendons or ligaments. After getting the results back the doctor revealed that I had some bone spurs and a partially torn ligament. We decided that getting it scoped would be the best thing to do. I got operated on two-weeks later, and four-weeks after surgery I bounced back and started my football training. When I felt like things were turning for the better I got really sick with mono. This was a real setback and put me out of commission for over a month. This only left me with a month before football camp started. I worked very hard for the next month but still didn't feel like I was completely ready. The first week of camp I felt good and understood the schemes of the offense. Then we had an inter-squad scrimmage and I was one of the leading rushers as a quarterback. Our coach, Jim Parady, did not like the fact that I wouldn't think twice about running with the ball.

That night after meetings he approached me and implied he wanted me to change positions and play receiver. He felt my athleticism and the demand for receivers would be my quickest way to get on the field. I talked about the situation to my father, and he was more upset than I was. Quarterback was a position that I had a great deal of success at and he thought I was adapting to the college game just fine. I decided to make the change and knew it would be easier mentally but physically the cutting was irritating my ankle.

The travel list came out for our season opener against Georgetown and I was confident I was making the trip. They decided to take a couple of seniors that would never play, but they felt it was a loyalty thing. I felt this was ludicrous because I was simply had more to offer the team. I did not handle that situation well and blew up on my position coach and asked Coach Parady how he evaluated talent. At this point I was sure I was going to transfer and made calls to Richmond.

The following week we were playing St. Peters in Jersey City and I made the travel list. We dominated the entire game; Coach Parady called my name to go in. At this point my head was not in it and I really did not want to stay at Marist College. I started jogging from the bench to cross the sideline, collapsed, and started screaming cramp. My buddy who was the place kicker started stretching me and was laughing. I didn't really have a cramp but I was aware that once I crossed that sideline a year of my eligibility was gone. That next day I broke the news to Coach Parady that I would be red-shirting. A week later, I left the football team and started playing basketball. Our point guard Bo Larigan hurt his shoulder and with lack of guards I felt this would be the best decision. That season I played in fourteen games and really refined my skills.

Right before finals that year, one of the assistant basketball coaches asked me my plans for the following year. Then he said, "Sean you should just play basketball." Scott Rumsey who was an assistant football coach told him that I would never see the field. I laughed it off and said silently to myself: "More fuel for the fire". When grades came out I was notified I made the Dean's List for the fourth straight semester. My freshman year in college I lost a total of twenty-five pounds. The following year I complained time and time again to the college café regarding the quality of food served. They eventually got tired of my complaints and started cooking me special meals. Thanks to the Marist College café staff my sophomore year I managed to maintain the weight I put on over the summer.

10

RENEWED INSPIRATION

"When one door closes, another opens; but often we look so long at the closed door that we do not see the one which has opened for us."

—Helen Keller

The summer going into my junior year on July 14, 1999 I met my soul mate, Krista Lantych. Words cannot describe the connection we share. She believed in me when I doubted, and has stood by me through thick and thin. I simply could not imagine my life without her. I am not sure I would have followed the path I did if it were not for her. She came into my life when I needed support and wanted to separate myself from negative influences. That summer I decided to train like I never did before.

That summer is when I became more of a student of the game. Watching films daily and trying to learn different techniques that would put me in a situation to be more successful. My father started tossing me bricks to toughen up my hands. As a receiver catching a football is all about concentration and by doing the brick drill, lack of concentration will result in loosing a tooth or maybe the family jewels. I focused more on heavy squats and other Olympic lifts that would help increase my power to make me faster. My brother Eric was my human jugs machine and used to throw me the football from close ranges using different combinations of velocity. My girlfriend Krista is extremely knowledgeable on the human body. She was a competitive gymnast for thirteen years at Yellow Jacket Gymnastics Club and placed at the national level on the uneven bars numerous times. She took me through complicated and challenging stretching sessions, which left me hobbling around. By the end of the summer she had me doing splits all the way down to the floor and bridges with the greatest of ease. In addition I played a ton of basketball. In fact our team, Northeast, won the gold medal in the Bay State Games Collegiate Division.

Entering my third year of college pre-season camp, I was confident that things would be different this season, even if I didn't have some of the coaches in my corner. Each year at Marist, the first day of pre-season workouts was focused on speed testing, in which the coaches timed us in the forty-yard dash. My first two years I ran 4.7's, and I knew that would not cut it with the receiver position. That year I ran a 4.5 and gave them a sneak preview of what was going to be showcased when we took the field. Once I got on the field, it became quite apparent that I was the most improved player on the team. During our inter-squad scrimmage I was the leading receiver and was working in with the first team. I was still not sure if I would be able to outplay the politics. Just like in other areas of life, people face obstacles they cannot surpass for reasons they could spend their entire lives trying to figure out. Playing on the basketball team was held against me because I did not participate in the football winter workouts.

When the depth charts came out two days before the first game I was listed as the third down receiver, which didn't quench my thirst but gave me hope. We ran the pro-set and ran the ball about seventy percent of the time. The first game no balls came my way and this made me frustrated. The following week we played high powered Duquesne and I caught two balls. The next three weeks, I barely played and was getting pretty down. I set up a meeting with Coach Parady to let him know how I felt.

The following week against Wagner College I had two catches and one was on fourth and long to set up the game winning field goal. At this point I thought maybe I had earned a starting position, but instead my position coach Ken Barger, decides to relieve me of my 3rd down receiver job. Because I was an underclassman and the player I was competing against was a senior. Here I am trying to get to the next level and have to try to digest news like that. Finally I told myself I couldn't work with this guy. I'd been busting my hump in practice, playing consistent and being very easy to coach. I started to believe it was time to give it up and move on to life after football. Right after meetings, I got really emotional and called home and revealed to my mother that I had quit. She was in complete shock that those words came out of my mouth. She said, "Sean, stop crying. No Stellato is a quitter. Don't give anyone the satisfaction of seeing that you are hurting because once they see that they will know they got the best of you." "Michael Jordan was cut from his high school basketball team because his coach saw nothing special. He wasn't good enough. How tragic would it have been for him and the world had he responded to the disappointment by quitting? Michael's message is compelling-hang in there. Nobody defines the limits of what you can become but you!" (*The New Toughness Training for Sports, by James E. Loeir*)

I didn't end up leaving the team, and finished up the season with 5 catches but I was ready to leave the program. By season end, I was named to the MACC All-Academic Team. I only played in ten games that basketball season but I was content and realized I was behind two excellent guards, Sean Kennedy and Rick Smith. I looked at the positives of the situation: I stayed in shape and got to compete at a high level and do some traveling. When I was on break from college and when Rick Brunson of the Chicago Bulls and Scoonie Penn of the European league came home I was called to play pick up games.

I got my release, which would allow me to talk to other schools, and I did talk to U-Albany and U-Richmond. Both schools revealed that I would lose the year I red-shirted and only have one year of eligibility. I talked it over with my parents and came to the conclusion that academically I had a 3.6 grade point average and was very situated at Marist. Not to mention that all my classes transferring was another issue because some might not transfer. I decided to stay at Marist and made a promise to myself that I would get so good and outwork everybody by so much that they would have no choice but to let me play.

I made a big decision and moved off campus to isolate myself from any distractions. It was very hard for me to get any work done in the dorms. Some of things I witnessed in the dorms would not sit to well with parents that will be sending their children to college in the future. I am the type of student with a Type-A personality who can only work diligently in complete silence. I practically lived in a private study room in the library. The dorm life was not for me and my immune system would often break down. I spent a lot of nights in the school infirmary. My senior year I moved in with Phil Paterno and Justin Greenblum, two ambitious kids from Staten Island that I had a lot in common with. They both had a vision on what they wanted to do with their lives and had a drive to succeed. One was studying to become a doctor and the other was studying to become a lawyer. The question I kept on asking myself going into the summer, was I ready mentally to conquer the eventual task at hand? "Dreams are created in the mind but live in the heart, the time is now." This quote has helped me stay focused to this day.

11

SPEED KILLS! SURVIVAL OF THE FASTEST

"If you can imagine it, you can achieve it, if you can dream it, you can become it."

—Anonymous

As you move up the ladder of organized sports, the higher you go, the more you have to deal with specific stereotypes. In football, size is a very important attribute especially when the player is not big. If you're labeled "too small," it stays with you forever. Speed is another important area. The reputation of being "too slow" will greatly hinder your opportunity of getting the chance to play at a higher level. At this point in my career, I needed to separate myself from my competition. Obviously I wasn't getting many opportunities on the field at Marist, but I stayed true to my principles, was always very optimistic, and felt like I was almost at the other side of the rainbow.

Two weeks into my summer workouts I started getting severe lower back pains. They were so bad I couldn't even sleep. I went for an MRI and the doctor diagnosed me with a disc problem, which would keep me out of the weight room and off the track for at least a month. The only activity I could do was water training. Therefore Krista and I improvised for the month of June and did everything you could think of to improve my skills while in the pool. I don't think she will ever forget the first time that she saw me swim laps at the Salem State College pool. Lets just say that I never had swimming lessons as a child and she thought I was going to drown, we still joke about it.

After I got cleared from the doctor to start weight training. I basically needed a football miracle. I was well behind and finally started to feel healthy at the beginning of July. This is when Ron Jones the ultimate personal trainer came into my life. The first time I met with Ron was at a local high school. He worked me out for two hours, and to this day I believe that workout might be the most pain I ever endured in a single workout. As I drove home I said to myself: "This is what I need to be successful this season." I finally had the guidance and expertise of someone who knew what speed was all about. Ron introduced me to training regiments I never dreamed of. Running barefooted on astro-turf, down hill, up-hill sprinting, pushing cars in neutral, using the parachute, bungee cord, pulling a sled with eight-five pounds, and running in beach sand.

Ron's philosophy was that it didn't matter how big you were, could you still run and make plays on the field. He was building more power and explosiveness in my legs and turning white muscles fiber into red fast twitch fibers. Running one forty at 4.5 was not that impressive to him, he wanted me to be able to run eight to ten at 4.5. Ron is simply amazing and put countless hours into my training sessions, I am forever grateful for everything he has done for me. When the city clock struck noon on a hot July day and Ron would say, "Dominate the workout in these conditions and games would be like a walk in the park." Day in and day out he pushed me to the limit. The track used to get so hot it would literally burn my feet and when I took off my shoes my socks would be full of blood and torn skin.

Up until my senior and fifth year season I worked hard but the training I was doing with Ron was just about unbearable. Ron completely increased my threshold for pain. My mother used to be scared every time I went to train with him because numerous times I got heat stroke and would come home sick as a dog. Throughout the summer all I could think about was a starting position. I kept that vision with me at all times. I kept reminding myself to: "Listen to your critics…they will keep you focused and innovative." That quote has helped me feed a lot of fuel to the fire.

The training that I experienced in those two summers made two weeks of two practices a day easy. My motto was if you wanted to be the best, you had to train like the best. I truly believed that there was not a player that went through the Marist football program that trained as hard as I did. Even though I wasn't awarded any hardware like some others were for working out, many of my teammates knew what I stood for and the commitment and dedication I displayed at all times. With Ron helping to improve my strength in my legs and teach me the proper techniques on how to run, I was ready for the forty-yard dash at the start of pre-season camp before my senior year. I proved it and ran a 4.49.

The coaches quickly noticed the benefits of my stepped-up Ron Jones training routine. I was not only fast but also had excellent endurance, which was made apparent during conditioning at the end of practice. This is when I would out run my competition by twenty yards. This earned me a starting position but I still had to rotate series with another receiver. My first collegiate start I had an acrobatic 40-yard touchdown reception that opened a lot of eyes. Moments later in the end zone I got on one knee and praised the man above who made this all possible. I was starting to live my dream.

The breakthrough game of my college career came when we played Wagner College in the fourth week of the season. The game started off on a negative note for me. In the first half I ran a fade and blew past the defensive back; I was wide open and our quarterback threw me a bomb that looked like a sure touchdown. It would have been an 80-yard touchdown but it went right through my hands. That was the only ball that I ever dropped in college. I wanted to continue running into the locker room. At halftime, Coach Parady got on me but I got support from some of my teammates. The second half is when I rekindled my flame as a football player thanks to back-up quarterback John Corneliusen who replaced our injured starting quarterback. I ended up catching two touchdowns; one coming with five seconds left remaining to be the game winner.

From that game on, I continued to improve. I finished the season leading all receivers with yards per catch and touchdowns. That season I got more of an opportunity but my position coach was still holding me back, which left me unsatisfied. It was obvious that I improved with just five weeks of training from Ron and I couldn't even imagine where my ability would go with an entire summer. In the meantime I finished up a four-year basketball career but again our team was denied of making it to the NCAA tournament.

The second semester of my senior year is when I took my faith and spiritualism to a new and higher level. I met with Father La Morte at the College Chapel for the entire semester and had numerous meetings with him. This is when he broke down Christianity as a whole for me and helped me build my faith. Krista also helped me with certain areas in Christianity that I was not clear on. She is the kind of person that has a tremendous faith and belief however it is not apparent to everyone around her. That May at the end of the semester, I was baptized, received first communion and received my confirmation. This was a very touching experience that turned me into a man of faith.

That summer Ron and I worked together for twelve gruesome weeks. Physically and mentally I was in a position that I was a stranger to, prior to being taken under Ron's wing. The goal we set for the season was to get as many eye-catching highlights as possible to impress professional scouts. We both knew that I would be limited because the coaching staff would not make the commitment to me to label me as "the man."

One of the coaches was really not aware of the ins and outs of the receiver position. He was an alumnus of Marist Collage and played on the football team in his day. He favored certain receivers because of their ethnicity; it was quite obvious throughout the football program. He never showed you how to do things a certain way, which made it very hard on me. Fortunately our defensive backs coach was Larry Riley. He was a member of the Denver Broncos "orange crush" defense. When he worked with me I would try to be like a sponge around him and absorb everything.

That season there would be games where I would not see a single pass and would rotate so frequently that after a game I would be so energized and upset that I would go directly into the weight room or basketball court and let out my anger. The beginning of my fifth year the September 11th attacks occurred and put everything into perspective for me. Marist had five alums and one student perish in those attacks. No matter how discontented I would get after a game that season, a quick glance at a picture of the twin towers would change my mood in seconds. From that day on I would tell myself every morning, "Make the most out of every day that you're alive."

Throughout my college and prep school career when weekend football games rolled around I knew that my mom would replenish my food supply. She would not only bring me food but she would also bring me a big cooler of her home cooked food. You name it she would fit it in the cooler and make sure that they had enough room to put all the food in the car. She always made sure that I had more then enough food stashed in my room. I will be forever grateful for the way she took care of me.

The last game my fifth year season was home versus Siena. I felt very empty after that game and I knew that it was not the end of my football career. I wanted to go out in style but instead I rotated most of the game and didn't see one pass attempt come my way. Walking off Leonidoff Field for the last time November 17, 2001, provided me with sense of relief. As I look back at my collegiate football career I can honestly say I made the most out of every opportunity that was bestowed upon me. My approach to everything was 110 percent, seeing first hand others in my receiver's core get more of an opportunity was a little hard to swallow. However it instilled an ingredient of character and pride that no one could touch with a ten-foot pole not even a fake or hypocritical coach.

As a student, I grew each semester and graduated January 2002, cum laude. Making the Dean's List every semester of my collegiate career. I learned excellent social skills and was quite aware that the human capital I learned at Marist would bring me corporate success in the business world when the time would come. However for the time being I was still chasing my dream and no one would stop me from achieving my ultimate dream.

12

MY FOURTH QUARTER

"When you reach the end of your rope, tie a knot in it and hang on."

—Thomas Jefferson

The period between Thanksgiving and early December was a very nerve-racking period because I was waiting to hear from some professional teams. Every time my cell phone rang, I would keep my fingers crossed and say a quick pray. Finally on December 3, 2001, I got a call from the Carolina Rhino's, an Arena team. The coach Rod Miller indicated he liked what he saw on tape and wanted to offer me a contract. My heart almost came through my mouth. When I got off the phone I looked liked Jim Valvano did after his team won the 1982 National Championship, very emotional with no one to hug. The contract came the following Friday and my family and I were overwhelmed with joy. I owe a great deal of thanks to my roommate and football teammate, John Dalzell, who was a friend through college and helped me keep my faith.

I finished up college and got back into Salem, Massachusetts on December 19, 2001. Right when I walked in my mother told me that John Fourcade from the Florida Firecats/Arena Football 2 had called and left his number. Later that night I called him, and he sold himself and the situation in Florida pretty well. Coach Fourcade explained how he had played five seasons for the New Orleans Saints in the NFL and that he was in line to get a job with the New Orleans VooDoo the following season. It was then he offered me a contract to play in South Florida. I implied that I would get back to him shortly because I had to weigh out the pros and cons. After talking it over with my parents and Krista, I decided this was too good to pass up and contacted Coach Fourcade. Coach Fourcade sent the contract over-night and I signed immediately upon receipt. When I signed the contract my father as well as my brother Michael made it a point to be there for me.

The Florida Firecats was only Arena 2, which is the developmental league for the Arena League. However, I was going to play in one of the three professional football leagues in all of the United States of America. Deep down inside I wish I got the same opportunity as Wayne Chrebet and signed as a free agent. But when you come from a small school like Marist, you need a ton of breaks and I had not received any. I look at Chrebet and see a lot of similarities: we both are 5'9", 186 pounds, have come from 1-AA schools located in New York, are very family oriented people, had Grandmothers that will always be our true inspirations, and have special girlfriends that have been instrumental in our lives. Many athletes say Wayne Chrebet got lucky but, as I said before, "Luck is when preparation meets opportunity." He is a talented football player and deserves everything he has achieved. I was starting from the bottom of the ladder of professional football. Mental toughness was an important concept for me.

Bill Kipouras is a prestigious sports editor for one of the best-known newspapers that covers the Northeastern part of Massachusetts, The Salem Evening News. He has been writing about my football career since I was fourteen years old. He did a nice article on me when I signed with the Florida Firecats. He focused on my work ethic, character, and my complete circle of true believers (family & loved ones). Kip has been great to me over the years. He titled it "Stellato Fulfills Pro Football Dream."

I knew with the opportunity, the support from my loved ones and with my commitment to God I could make a smooth transition playing Arena football. I just wanted a chance to play in the pros. I am the type of person who if I get a crack; I'm going to turn it into Lake Ontario. Each year I refurbished my skills and made tremendous strides as a football player. I define overachiever. Many have told me from day one what I would never do. Those types of people never could understand they couldn't measure my heart or brain. I have fulfilled my dream and no one can ever take that away from me. Training with NFL players David Givens, Max Lane and Adam Young at a speed school was a great experience that winter.

On Krista's birthday, March 12, 2002, we took a twenty-five hour train ride down to Fort Myers, Florida. I fought the flu and a fever the entire way down. Krista took care of me the entire trip, ensuring that I took in enough water and medication to help me heal. She must have done something right because by the time we checked into the hotel I was doing sprints in the parking lot. The day after we arrived I contacted the coach and from that day on I was treated like a professional football player. He went out of his way to make me feel welcome, by buying us diner, lunch, trips to the beach, taking us to a Harlem Globe Trotters game and to Sanibel Island. Even though we were amazed by his generosity we knew that I would have to prove myself on the field. I kept my vision clear and stayed humble. I have never had anything handed to me in football and I knew that things were not going to change. I worked out daily ensuring I was on the top of my game.

At the first team meeting we had player introductions. I remember the two guys next to me standing up and saying their names: Magic Benton of University of Miami and Anthony Dixon of Marshall. Right then and there I realized playing was going to require my "grade A effort" night in and out. The following night we took the field and as I was stepping on the field, our public relations lady asked if Fox Sports could interview me. That caught me by surprise. My first couple of practices I had the jitters and dropped some catchable balls. That put me in hot water. After those first two days I was all about productivity and started playing like a fine-tuned pro. After the team started to make cuts I found myself barely sleeping because I knew it was going to be a close call. The head coach gave me his word, but that was not something he stayed true to because I was the last player released. This was a devastating blow that caused me a great deal of grief. The head coach indicated the decision was out of his hands and it had to do with my lack of arena experience. The general manager who owned the team knew I was fresh out of college and that it was going to take some time for me to make the transition. Apparently they had no patience for me. I guess when you are handed everything your entire life you have a different outlook on life then someone who has had to work for everything.

Anthony McKenzie who was one of my teammates in Florida really hit some interesting points and helped allow me to look at the entire ordeal from a different perspective. Anthony used to call me Rocky because he saw me doing some crazy exercises in the weight room and doing wind sprints at night in the parking lot. He knew how much I put into the game and he made this statement: "Channel as much effort into God that you do training and he will put you in the best possible situation." He hit the nail right on the head and from that day on God has been my anchor and has received one hundred percent of me.

A couple of days later I was training on my own, behind where the team was practicing and my position coach Bernard Edwards who played at Ohio State and had eight successful years in the Arena League approached me. He revealed that he knew what I was going through, that I caught a raw deal and was caught up in a numbers game. He said to keep my faith and that I had a future in this game.

He completely lifted me up and I don't think that he knew the impact he made on me by saying that and I never really got the opportunity to thank him. He then went on to tell me that he had a friend who coached in Pensacola for another Arena 2 team. He said that he would do everything in his power to get me a workout. I touched base with the coach in Pensacola and he was upbeat about me going there.

It was a seventeen-hour bus trip to Pensacola. Let me tell you something, traveling by Greyhound is very demanding on you, especially when you have half your house with you. John Fourcade offered to fly me there but I figured the ride would be therapeutic. I was in Pensacola for about a week and faced even more adversity. I worked out for two days and barely got any repetitions. They even scrimmaged the entire practice on a Wednesday and I didn't see one repetition. The only thing they could evaluate me on was that I won every gasser I ran. After those practice their assistant coach came up to me and told me "We think you're a good player but we can't use you." The one positive that came out of me going to Pensacola was I met a quarterback named E.T. from Albany, Georgia. He had the strongest arm I have ever seen and played a couple of seasons of minor league baseball. He drove me all the way to Albany's Greyhound station.

This is where I hit rock bottom and got really emotional. I must have called the head coach of the Carolina Rhinos about five times and left five messages. I assumed he was screening my calls because I didn't sign with him a few months earlier. I walked into the bathroom and looked at myself in the mirror as I watched the tears running down my face. I said out loud, "Keep your head up. It just wasn't meant to be." As I was walking up to the clerk to purchase my ticket to Boston, which was a forty-two hour ride, my phone started ringing. It was Rod Miller the head coach of the Carolina Rhinos, and he welcomed me up to Greenville, South Carolina, for a two-day workout. I accepted his offer and was on my way traveling through the night.

The entire three weeks I spent in Greenville felt like three years. From the first day to the last, it was like beating a dead horse. I was working hard and making plays but just could not see the field. I was designated to the practice squad and this is where I met one of my closest friends, Mike 'hard hitting' Summers. Mike is one of the best athletes I ever played with and is a very sincere person who should be playing in the NFL, but had some tough breaks. Mike said, that being one of the only white boys on the team was hurting me because they were pro black. That really made me think, and after paying closer attention I got the same impression. That was mind boggling because I pride myself on diversity.

The living arrangements were horrendous. We nicknamed the place we were staying, "Spanish Harlem" and "The Jungle." We had seven players staying in a three-bedroom apartment with no beds or furniture. Mike actually slept in a walk-in closet. Nick Johnson who was the team's offensive specialist did supply some laughs with the magic tricks he performed occasionally. He could make a dollar float in the air. It was pretty crazy. Despite the similarities with David Copperfield, he couldn't make the cockroaches or spiders disappear. I used to get so delirious from lack of sleep that I would try to put my travel bags together to make a bed but that wouldn't last because I would soon find myself back on the floor. In addition, hunger was very common. I am an athlete who treats his body like a brand new Lexus. Jerry Rice, Walter Payton and Ricky Henderson are all athletes who took care of their bodies and played considerably longer than the average athlete is accustomed to. This ride was very rocky but I was building character, a vital element that will help make my transition into the corporate world easier.

One morning as I began my daily prayer session I got a phone call from Jeff Brohm who was the head coach of the Louisville Fire, which is another Arena 2 team. He told me that he received a call on my behalf and wanted to see some film because his team was 0–4 and lacking depth at the receiver position. I got the tape out and put in a word for my buddy Mike who was a defensive specialist. Three days later I got the okay from Brohm. Mike was also invited, which was great because we took the trip together. It was like God telling me that he still had a plan for me in football. I never considered it a knock on my ability that I didn't make it with Florida or Carolina. I came out of Marist, which was a small school. This was a whole new ballgame: a narrow fifty-yard field with an eight-yard end zone and a very fast pace on Astroturf with walls that don't give. Leaving Greenville, also known as the "The Jungle," was like getting out of jail, but it was another long, tiresome, nagging journey with hunger pains for twelve hours through the night on the infamous greyhound bus. If I had to do it over again, I would have taken the same path. I made friends in South Carolina that will last a lifetime. I did a lot of soul searching for the duration of the bus ride and came to the conclusion that if I didn't find my niche in Louisville it was time to head home. My parents were concerned about my living conditions and were feeling my pain. Krista never lost her faith in me and stood by me the entire time, I did not let a day go by without talking to her.

Louisville, Kentucky was the last spot I thought I would end up. Prior to going there I never knew how big a football city it was. The only thing I really knew about Louisville was Churchill Downs where the Kentucky Derby was held. Jeff Brohm had a very respectable athletic resume and was like a junior Rick Pitino in the area. Jeff played five seasons in the NFL, was Steve Young's backup in San Francisco, and was a member of the San Diego Charger's 1995 Super Bowl team. Coach Brohm was very blunt and said, "Make plays and you will play."

May 13, 2002, was my first practice and from that point on I promised myself I would not worry about the things that I couldn't control. I needed to really focus on perfecting being explosive, running textbook routes, and catching the ball. I was trying to compensate for the lack of Arena experience and areas that I felt the coaches might think I was lacking in. The playbook was very complex and required more plays to learn than any of the previous teams. After each practice I would run the stadium steps that overlooked the city of Louisville. The sun was setting in the horizon and each step I took was brining me closer to my dream of running through the tunnel at Freedom Hall. The team's defensive coordinator, Tommy Johnson, was a starter for the Alabama Crimson Tide's 1992 National Championship team, had two years in the NFL, and played four successful seasons in the Arena League, became my mentor. He broke the game down to a science demonstrating all the key angles that needed to be taken to be successful in the game; this helped me become a student of the Arena game.

After a very productive first week I didn't get the nod to play while Mike Summers did. This was heart wrenching considering I came up to Louisville the same time he did. Numerous players thought I should have especially Jerry Dorsey a wide receiver/defensive back who the year before signed with Seattle Seahawks. The following day Dorsey came by the apartment before the team was departing to Illinois and gave me a small book called *The Prayer of Jabez*. He implied that the book helped him when he was trying to make the Seahawks roster. The book, in a nutshell helps the reader break through to the blessed life. I read it religiously and memorized the prayer:

> **"Oh, that you would bless me indeed, enlarge my territory, that your hand would be with me, that you would keep me from evil, and that I may not cause pain"** (*The Prayer of Jabez, Bruce Wilkinson*).

During practice I would catch balls and would be running up field saying the prayer in my head. The following week I had all pistons firing, knew the playbook inside and out, and was turning the defensive backs around. This is where I saw the mountain and now knew it wasn't too steep to climb. Coach Johnson approached me and said, "I am going to bat for you to sign." Sure enough the next day I signed.

May 31, 2002, is a night I will cherish for the rest of my life. We were hosting the team I came from the Carolina Rhinos. As I got ready to run through the tunnel onto the field I got chills throughout my body and started recalling events that had happened in the past. Hearing phrases from Mike Fisher, Warren Arms, Ken Barger, Chris Vallozi and Jim Parady all helped add more fuel to my fire. A special thanks to all of them for doubting my ability. They made me even stronger. I saw my parents cheering, my Krista's beautiful smile, my brothers giving each other high five's, Ron Jones just doing his best impression of Mr. Miyagi at the end of Karate Kid smiling, and my inspiration Owa on my shoulder being one of my guardian angels. Life is all about being happy and fulfilling your dreams. I started the journey eighteen years earlier when I first put the pads on, to one day become a professional athlete.

That game against Carolina was the team's first win. On my first play in the game I caught my first ball as a professional athlete. That season structured my life in a different way than prep school and college had. It gave me a first class lesson in the real world. I traveled to places I would have never imagined going and played in front of 10,000 fans during our home games. I learned that the Louisville fans are loyal and stay true even when you don't win. The biggest joy I get from being a professional athlete is the fans, especially the younger ones. September 21, 2001, my fifth year of college, we were playing Florida Atlantic at Pro Player Stadium in Miami. We were staying at the same hotel as the Oakland Raiders. The local newspaper did an article prior to the game and my name was mentioned as the team's leading receiver. Jerry Rice used to be one of my idols. I felt it would be neat if he signed the article so I tried to track him down. I approached him with the article and he looked at it and walked off. That made me sick and I lost a ton of respect for him. From that day on I promised myself I would never deny someone a signature. After each game it's a league rule that all fans are allowed access to the field for pictures and autographs. This is where I get complete joy, seeing the excitement I can give a youngster by giving him or her an autograph, a glove, or a wristband. I was always the last player to leave the field after every game. One night after a game, a little girl approached me and introduced me to her cousin Dana; she whispered in my ear that he was five and his mom just passed from cancer. Being a mama's boy, my heart went out to him. My first instinct was to put myself in this kids shoes, what I asked myself was what would make me smile: an autographed t-shirt. I ran into the locker room and grabbed a shirt and signed it. When I approached him I put it on him, he gave me a big kool-aid smile. His uncle came up to me and said, "Thanks, that's the first time he has smiled since his mother passed." That's what life is all about, touching someone else's life. God was enlarging my territory; *Prayer of Jabez* was in full effect.

Through football, I feel I can be an inspiration to other athletes who face many obstacles and help them overcome adversity. I think I'm living proof that if you work hard enough good things will happen. My ultimate dream was to play in the NFL but as one of my goals was to play pro football, as one door closes another opens, God only knows what is in store for me.

I wish things could have materialized a little better that season but what it came down to was that I got two seasons in one. Playing college football that fall and professional football in the spring and summer. In addition, I got the key Arena experience I needed. Jeff Brohm is a man I have the utmost respect for. Not only did he help me to fulfill a dream but also he gave me an opportunity, which was something no other pro-coaches would do. The *Prayer of Jabez* worked its miracles in Louisville, thanks to Dorsey coming into my life and faith. I am truly blessed and believe God has had a plan for me pertaining to football. I feel I can glorify God by playing football. In other words, I can bring more athletes closer to him. Many athletes are always in the limelight and are surrounded by temptation like drugs, alcohol, and sex. Once I met Krista, who was sent to me as one of God's children that helped protect me from the deamons and overcome temptation. I grew into the Christian that I wanted to become.

My parents asked me if I was mad that the Florida Firecats went to the Championship. I was not because it just showed that I got released from a good team and contributed to them winning a championship. When caught up in politics and a numbers game you usually lose. This is the dark side of sports that depletes the passion for football from many athletes that hope to reach the highest level they can possibly play. I was not sure if this would end my career like it had for so many others. As an athlete, there is a tendency to observe players to compare your game or to pick up different techniques. After seeing some of the top players in the league and seeing techniques used, I had no doubt in what I could do given the chance.

My parents, two brothers, and Krista have been with me through every segment of the journey. Every level I played has been for my family, teammates, and fans. I wanted to take them on a ride that no theme park could ever offer. I truly believe I have done that for my parents. I have helped give to them a little fountain of youth along the way. My parents never took vacations because of me playing all over the place. They had few opportunities for getaways.

In the meantime it was back on the Greyhound but this time it was to go home on a twenty-four hour bus ride. This is when I mapped out a seven-month grand plan that focused on exhausting every possible football avenue. I have a fear of flying just to let you know why I would put myself through these bus rides. Louisville Fire made it clear that they wanted to re-sign me for the following season, but would they stay true to their word? Tommy Johnson left me with the statement that he would take me wherever he ended up, but would he stay true to his principles?

13

FINAL DRIVE

◆

OVERTIME

"The difference between a successful person and others is not the lack of strength, not a lack of knowledge, but rather a lack of will."

—Vince Lombardi

Not everyone is born with every athletic tool or height needed to succeed in sports. Then again, not everyone has a certain passion to excel, the work ethic to do it, or the support system to make it all possible. Having these three key elements with me at all times has enabled me to keep my faith, not only when things looked up but also when difficulties were knocking at my door. I always believed that someone could be bigger, someone could be faster and stronger, but nobody was going to ever outwork me. In years past I worked hard and knew I needed to make the most out of the opportunity that came my way.

My personal trainer Ron and I put together a blueprint of seven months of speed and strength workouts that would help me physically and put me in a position that my body had never experienced before. I took ten days off and then it was like how Marvelous Marvin Hagler trained before facing top contender's "total isolation". Hagler was an excellent pro-boxer and used to isolate himself from people when he was getting ready for a fight. Due to playing basketball I never had more than three months to train for football, so all this extra training made me feel very optimistic that positive things were waiting for me in the horizon.

My schedule consisted of wakeup at 6:00A.M and an appointment with my sports therapist, Mike Lovett, who took care of me five days a week. If it were not for Mike constantly fixing the little tweaks, I would have never been able to train like I did day in and day out. Mike went out of his way for me ensuring that he took care of all my aliments. Every morning I would eat a light breakfast and consume one gallon of water. I never step on the track or football field without being totally hydrated. I would spend three rigorous hours at the track. Mondays and Thursdays would be strength workouts which consisted of 150, 200, and 300 yard sprints, pulling a weighted sled which would be up to 85-pounds on a harness, parachute, hills, beach sand sprints, and all my offensive related drills, catching balls or bricks, running all my routes. Tuesdays, Wednesdays, and Fridays would be all speed workouts: 100, 80, 60, 40 yard sprints and skill improvement. I would run on the treadmill backwards at 6 miles per hour. People would watch me in awe and make statements like "I can't run that fast forward." Immediately after the track workout I would eat a packed lunch and it would be off to Bally's Total Fitness. This is where I would spend three hours working on my body while lifting weights, doing 1,000 sit-ups and 1,000 reps of jump rope. Every night Krista and I would work on my flexibility, which is something I take pride in, especially being able to do my left leg split all the way down to the floor. After each workout I would take twenty minutes in a Jacuzzi to relax and meditate. I spent thirty to thirty-five hours a week for seven months training for the 2003 season and I did not play in one game. I was under contract but was on the inactive list. I waited tables, bartended and did personal training to pay some of my bills.

The month of September, I exhausted every Arena possibility and sent out tapes and articles, any small thing that would give coaches a better idea of my character. Two teams responded the New York Dragons and the Indiana Firebirds.

I went to an open workout in Hicksville, Long Island on September 21, 2002. There were over two hundred participants from all over the country and the Dragons coaches' objective was to cut it to fifteen by the end of the workout. Every two hours they would make cuts. The workout started at 9:00 A.M. and lasted until 4:00 P.M. Let's say I made the most out of my opportunity that day and was one of fifteen players chosen to attend their mini-camp. That day I was in the zone and caught every ball in my vicinity. There was a problem because the next day my Godson Troy who is also my nephew was getting baptized, and the obligation for the Godfather in the Catholic religion is to be present. I talked to Coach Gregory, the head coach of the Dragons, and he okayed it. Coach gave me his word I would be brought back for another workout. When I left I felt empty because I was walking away from a chance to go against their starters and earn a spot in the Dragons training camp. I talked to Aaron Garcia who is the Joe Montana of the Arena League and he gave me some very good feedback and liked my skills. The following week the Dragons had an article on their website which they mentioned my name. Coach Gregory stated "We seen enough positive work on Sean and will work him out in the near future." That made me even more motivated and determined but Coach Gregory was not too honorable to his word since he never brought me back. This started to leave me with the impression that you can never take a coach's word. I am grateful for my family and realize that I made the right decision to be there for my nephew, family easily outweighs everything else in life.

My next workout came November 14, in Westminster, Maryland. Krista and I made the trip by car down to Maryland. The workout was a private one and consisted of the 40-yard dash, 20-yard shuttle, and one on ones. There were only about ten athletes there. The workout was strictly a learning experience and I didn't get picked up. After the workout I was depressed due to the fact that I had been training rigorously for three months and I was ready to make my mark on the Arena field.

I kept in contact with Coach Brohm and he verbally committed that he was going to re-sign me and would get me out the contract after the Thanksgiving holiday. Two weeks later he resigned to take a position at his Alma-Mata the University of Louisville. Dorsey called me and hinted that Tommy Johnson was the front-runner for the job. That sounded good to me because of the commitment Tommy made to me. In the meantime it was time to turn up the workouts and take all my frustration out on my training. Worrying is putting faith in fear. Residing in the Boston area there is a lack of resources for athletes like myself trying to climb the ladder of professional sports. You can only manage so much in twenty-degree weather or on a track/field covered with snow.

From mid-December to mid-January the area got hit with a good amount of snow. Crazy me had a few more weeks pulling the eighty-pound weighted sled and could only pull it outside. After each snowfall I would go to Bishop Fenwick High School with Krista and I would shovel fifty yards up the field and five yards wide. We look back at this and laugh, Krista jokes that I got hit in the head too much in football. I was even more determined and was not going to let a little inclement weather stop me even though I had so much gear on I looked like the abominable snowman.

That off-season I really tried to become more of a student of the Arena game. Arena football is all about angles, if you can master angles you will be in a category with the likes of 'Touchdown' Eddie Brown or Hunkie Cooper. Those two are household Arena Football names. I studied the films of the games that I played in the year before. Since NBC had bought into the league with the NFL, games were televised every Sunday, my father taped those games and I would get new film sessions weekly.

That December my brother Michael who was the head coach of the St. Mary's Spartans football team asked me to be the guest speaker for the evening. I worked on the presentation for three weeks and wrote out twenty-five pages and then condensed it down to note cards. After the presentation some people came to the conclusion that my next calling should be a motivational speaker. Not only did I move many that night I made my message clear and simple: "Don't let anyone discourage you from going after your goals and dreams."

Mid-January, Wally English was named head coach of the Louisville Fire, and Tommy Johnson implied that the ball was out of his court, but he felt he could at least get me into training camp. At this point I became very perturbed and decided to contact the Green Bay Blizzard and Norfolk Nighthawks. Green Bay liked my film but was aware Louisville still had my rights and could not talk to me until I got released. Norfolk told me to keep quiet because they were going to request a trade for me. The trade went through two days before Coach Johnson made the statement "Your contract is going in the mail tomorrow." I didn't know what to believe, I started to have mixed emotions, but what it came down to was that all I wanted to do was play football. Coach Johnson revealed weeks later that Norfolk wanted me real bad and gave up two players for me.

At this point my friend Ken Farrar who was with the NFL's Baltimore Ravens for the 2002 training camp did not get allocated to NFL-Europe, and I played Jerry Maguire for a day. Norfolk sent Ken a contract. A week after that I got my close friend and former Louisville Fire teammate Mike Summers a contract.

I was on my last phase of training and it got even more intense. When I train I constantly visualize myself in a game situation. I constantly talk to myself especially when I start feeling fatigued. The drive that I have honestly is borderline of being completely crazy. One morning as I walked into Bally's the receptionist came up to me and said, "Sean some lady came up to me and described a person and it sounded like you, then she asked if the person was mentally challenged." I walked off laughing because she obviously did not know what intense football

training is all about. I am the type of athlete that will do whatever it takes to max-
imize every bit of energy I have. The only way that I will improve is by mastering
every workout. When I get fatigued I often think about what my competition is
doing at that very moment. That thought alone will put me in a state of mind
where I will overcome any obstacle. Wayne Chrebet did it, why can't I? This is a
player that I respect so much because I can identify his style with mine and the
simple fact we are both complete underdogs. I appreciate Chrebet, Doug Fluite,
and Walter Payton so much not just because they have been consistent, but also
because the tremendous amount of work they put into their training and preparation even after reaching the pinnacle of their profession. All three are completely
unique in their own way and have made significant contributions to the game.
After reading Walter Payton's book *Never Die Easy*, I had a good cry for myself
because he was not only the greatest football player ever but he also touched
thousands of lives. He took all his fine assets that he displayed on the field and
utilized them outside the game. Thousands of families were able to celebrate
Christmas because of him. Walter Payton was a true icon for every football
player. This might sound corny but before I start a demanding workout I will
often yell out his name to let him know how much I appreciate what he's done
for the game.

By beginning of March 2003, I was like a fined tuned machine and as ready as
ever. Coach Frazier who was the head coach of the Nighthawks called me, and we
had some good rapport. He was very enthusiastic and wanted this to be my breakout season. Something crazy happened the day I headed down to Virginia, I got
the flu. Exactly one year to the day I was sick when I headed down to Florida. I
felt bad for Krista because she was making the trip and when I'm sick I am like
Frank the Crank.

The following week we had team physicals and were issued equipment. The
next day Coach Frazier set up a meeting with me. The first thing he said was
"Sean your fucking groin is killing you." I looked at him like he was on drugs. He
said, " From here on out anyone asks, your groan is messed up. This will keep
you out of the numbers game and keep you around." Norfolk had their mind
made up before I got there what their plans were for me. Some idea he had for a
breakout season.

Two days later Ken left camp and told me his head wasn't in it. After having a
heart to heart talk with Mike Summers he came to the conclusion that coach
brought in his own boys and he wasn't ready to play games so he left also. Mike
said, "I don't mind competing and working hard but not even with your work
ethic could you outwork politics. Mike saw it coming before I did. That week

there was a good article written in my hometown paper labeled "Stellato's Dream leads to Norfolk." Bill Kipouras quoted Ken Farrar, " Sean is holding his own. It's tough because he's been bounced around. But he has a great work ethic. If half the players in this country had half his heart, they'd be all-pros. Sean's been training like Jerry Rice for the past seven-months." That was very nice of Ken to make those statements. Coming from a former NFL player that meant a lot especially knowing that he has been around the best and knows what I'm all about. I pride myself on work ethic

For two weeks I was put on the "physically unable to perform" list though I was as healthy as could be. This exempted me from both scrimmages, and I was only allowed to participate in four practices. I had to watch players that weren't nearly as good as me receive unlimited opportunities. The skill guys were mainly local guys who played with the team for the past couple of seasons. Don't get me wrong; they had a couple of solid receivers. The organization made a big deal out of one of their receivers who was a local player. It was his fourth season on the team. He was lazy, out of shape, and slow. He was very complacent in Arena 2 which is a league that players play in for a season or two and build themselves up to make the jump to Arena or a higher level of football. It's not to make it a career and take away someone else's opportunity.

March 29, 2003, each player met with the entire staff and received their assessments. Things really got hot when I was in the room. My big question was: How would you have felt if you trained like you were going to the Olympics for seven months, got traded from a team that would have at least let you show what you could do, and only got to participate in four practices during camp? Coach Hill who was the offensive coordinator starting yelling at me, saying I looked at everyone in the face except him, which was a lie because he had his head down the entire time I spoke because he knew he made a promise which he did not keep. At this point Coach Frazier said that if I stuck around and worked hard he would play me. So I requested the Mohegan game, which would be a homecoming for me because they are located in Connecticut. The following day before practice he approached me and said "You can't hold me accountable for what I said because It matters where we are as a team as we approach that game." I wanted to punch this guy out. One issue I could not digest was why did Norfolk bring me in? Was it because the year before they wanted me bad and I signed with Florida; I guess I will never know.

I immediately called Tommy Johnson at Louisville and he said hang tight and use them for reps, which will keep you close to the game. God will let you know when it's time to move on. I stuck around for a week and couldn't swallow my pride anymore. The entire ordeal was overwhelming, thinking about all that training made my mind go every which way.

The Cincinnati Swarm was another team that showed interest in me before the season but knew my situation was complicated with Louisville having my rights. After touching base with Chris McKeown and getting the invite, I packed up my car and headed to Cincinnati. The next day I received some great news, or so I thought, Tommy Johnson replaced Wally English as head coach of the Louisville Fire. I was ecstatic this was God's sign for me to head back to my mentor. That night I contacted Coach Johnson and congratulated him and got right to the point: "When can I come?" He gave me some bogus excuse that he had to talk to the general manager and to get back to him. When I got back to him he said Dave Arnold the general manager didn't okay it. So I told him I would come for a two-a-day to show him how much I improved. He had the audacity to say he didn't have enough equipment. Those remarks broke my heart. Here's a man I looked up to, he took me under his wing the year before, kept in contact with me all winter, helped me with my understanding of God and then totally contradicts himself. To make matters worse he tried to get Mike Summers down there and Mike asked about me. Tommy remarks, "Sean is not good enough to play here right now." I learned the hard way that he was only a preacher and did not care about my best interests.

My next move was to go to Cincinnati. Driving through the mountains of West Virginia I pulled over to eat lunch. The views were breathtaking and all I could think of was when Owa first passed away. I was at the cemetery crying at her burial and an old man approached me and said, "Kid you have your entire life in front of you and whatever you want to do in this lifetime it's out there just go get it." All I wanted was an opportunity. I was seeing a view that went on for miles and I started to realize I could reach that final destination and there isn't a mountain that I cannot climb without God. I wanted to put those seven months of training to the test, just to see how much I improved. I would fight until I got that chance and if it didn't work out I would be at ease when I go to sleep at night. I will know in my heart that I have exhausted every possible avenue with 110% effort and I just came up short. The human capital (knowledge, skills, and abilities) I learned at Marist and my unparalleled work ethic would not let me down like so many coaches have.

Cincinnati was a learning experience, and I feel that God brought me there for a special reason. He brought two special people into my life Ryan Russell and BJ Paulus, two inspiring athletes that had strong faiths and a ton of ability but both were facing obstacles like myself. This is really where the politics of football made me realize that it might be time for a career change. My love for the game was being over shadowed by the system. At this point I felt my next calling would be a sports agent. Interacting with Ryan and watching his film left me with no doubt that he should have been drafted by an NFL team. Coming from a small school lowered his stock and made him get overlooked, not to mention being a minority and facing that racial barrier would not help his cause. I have made a couple of calls on Ryan's behalf and have started to work on putting together a package that will promote him. After two weeks of speed workouts, prayer sessions with BJ and lots of Mexican food, it was time to move on. I was staying on a couch at one of the assistant coaches house who had three kids who could of stared in the movie Problem Child. I think they used to mix their cereal with Red Bull because of how hyper they were.

Green Bay Blizzard was another team that showed interest prior to the start of the season but with my rights being held up by Louisville they backed right off. I contacted Jose Jefferson the head coach of the Blizzard. He indicated that the team was 0–4 and struggling and there was plenty of opportunity if I came up. I decided that I put so much into the season why not give it one more chance. I'm not going to lie, the fact that the Packers organization was yards away was even more motivation to make the 600-mile trip. If it didn't work here it would be time to change careers. I looked at it like this; I was getting very knowledgeable on reading maps.

I lay in bed staring at the walls, hearing the sounds of heavy wind from Lake Michigan brush against the windows. The clock said ten minutes until four, and I'm saying to myself z flex right slot blast 55 slot option, x-read. I've got to understand the offense or I will never play. I need to be mentally sound because Coach Jefferson has no tolerance for mental lapses. The secondary is playing cover two, hammer, I need to find the area for the dig read. I need to electrify the crowd; it's all a slight opportunity away." Nights like this have been very common for me as I try to find my niche in professional football. Pro-football players need to have amnesia or they will find themselves looking back at past wrong turns they took that have had a negative impact on them.

May 28, 2003, I signed with the Blizzard but was going to get put on short-term injured reserve. Coach Jefferson sat on my contract for over two weeks and strung me along. What he did was wrong and it made me feel like I was taking a course in disappointment. The Green Bay situation was plain awful and as I look back at it, I think it was a blessing from God to get me out of there. The team was not that good and most of the team was made up of sororities, because of the way they had their feminine style clicks and constantly bashed each other. Most of the players set up a private meeting with the general manager to try to replace the coach; it was like a witch-hunt.

The following week Matt Hicks who was my quarterback in Louisville was brought in for a workout. I liked this because Matt threw a good ball and I know he would look for me. After the workout Matt got a call from the Memphis Xplorers to head down there to play because of injuries. Matt put in a word for me to Coach Matthews because a week earlier one of their receivers broke their leg.

Two days later I departed Green Bay with a few regrets but knowing I gave it everything I had. I arrived in Memphis, June 8.

I met with Coach Matthews who was the offensive coordinator; he had a solid six-year NFL career and gave me his word that he was all about honesty. He said it would be an uphill battle and it has been. After having some solid practices, the head coach, Danton Barto, signed me on June 19, 2003. This was two days before we were going to play the Louisville Fire. This was a game I wanted to play in but hours before the game I was put on the inactive list. I did make the trip up to Louisville with the team, and it was a tough experience because my heart still bleeds a little red and black which were the Fire's colors. We won which put our team one-step closer to making the playoffs.

My forty-five days in Memphis was a learning experience. I prepped for each practice like I was trying to impress NFL scouts. Playing in Memphis polished up my defensive back skills and instilled the confidence that I needed to be successful at the professional level.

An occurrence that bothered me deeply was that prior to the Green Bay Blizzard game, four starters got caught in the hotel smoking marijuana. The league rule states that the players should have been suspended or released but instead coach fined them. It's mind boggling to work as hard as I did in Memphis and not receive the opportunity to play while other players cut corners. The following Monday Coach handed out forms to the team that stated 'release' or 'remain' and that if it was up to him he would release them but it was our season so the decision was up to the players. Most of the team also smoked weed so you know the outcome of the vote. After this occurrence I started to question even more if professional sports was sending the right message to youngsters allowing players to abuse drugs and still get another chance. The NFL will only suspend a player for four games if they test positive for substance abuse (*NFL Collective Bargaining Agreement: 2003*).

"Your work ethic is incredible," Kevin Cobb, our starting defensive specialist, told me after a practice with the Memphis Xplorers. "I have been watching you, and everything you do is 110%. You should be playing here and you have the ability to be playing in the CFL and in the Arena League. All you are is an opportunity away." To hear that from a starter was very touching, especially from Kevin, who I looked up to and has played in the CFL, XFL and won an ESPY for Play of the Year in 1996 while playing for the University of Memphis when he returned a kickoff for a touchdown to beat U-Tennessee.

Before I departed home I had a sit down with Coach Barto and he said I was the team's most improved player and offered to re-sign me for the next year. Before I packed up to move for the twenty-two hour ride I bought a companion, puppy boxer named Sly. At this point my mind was going every which way. I still had the passion for the game but maybe it needed to be utilized as an agent. Mentally I was not sure if I could continue chasing the game as a player. As I drove into the sunset on Route 76, I decided that to live day by day and ask the Lord to either open more avenues with football as a player or completely close the door.

14

POLITICS & CHANGES IN FOOTBALL IN THE PAST 30 YEARS

"Keep away from people who try to belittle your ambitions. Small people always do that, but the really great make you feel that you, too, are great."

—Mark Twain

Politics often benefit individuals who become successful even though they do not work as hard as others. They are put into a beneficial situation because of their social class, and their connections control their destiny of others who are not as connected. Politics in sports are something that I can relate to all the way back to my freshman year of high school, with each occurrence becoming more recognizable. I have witnessed politics dictate the outcome quite often and many have been effected by political decisions. There were times when I stood back and waited for my name to be called to get the chance to prove myself, and there were occasions that my name was never called. I believe that I was another victim of politics of the game and did not get the chance simply because of my height, last name or the color of my skin.

As I moved up the ranks from high school, college, then to the pros I have noticed that the number of white athletes have diminished along the way and the ones who have not been dropped by the wayside have faced barriers that have made it very unlikely to get an opportunity. Are they not good enough or are they just labeled well before they even have a chance to showcase their skills on the field? Being stereotyped can often play a role in the lack of opportunities athletes receive. With the imbalance of racial makeups in professional sports, I wonder if this fact plays into the selection of athletes. It is apparent that African Americans do well in the context of percentages on professional teams. Is it genetics? Is it breeding? Or is it the perception that the black athlete is a better athlete? Are they? Most white professional football players today are offensive lineman, kickers, and quarterback's. In the basketball market the NBA are putting more Europeans in uniforms than white Americans. For many years football has brought my family and I tremendous excitement, however once I reached the professional level it was like a roller coaster ride leaving me extremely high on life one minute and then moments later feeling depressed and saddened. This is one of the dark sides of football that drains all the love for the game right out of you.

Growing up it used to make me sick to my stomach when I would see specific players holding out for large sums of money. After being played like a puppet by numerous organizations and first-hand seeing what happens if you get injured. I also witnessed the lack of job security and player longevity for professional football players, I can easily see why these athletes are cynical and hold out for more money. The public just doesn't understand the hard side of the business, yet alone the months of mental and physical preparation required and the complete sacrifices that have to be made. Many players that I have played with and went on to the NFL nicknamed it the "Not for long league". As driven and determined as I am I will never be able to outwork the politics of the game.

A former NFL Player Tim Green creates an interesting point in his book, *The Dark Side of the Game* pertaining to racism in the NFL. He states "If you ask black NFL players about the league they're in, almost to a man, you will find that they believe without a doubt that the racism they see throughout society is mirrored exactly in the NFL. Although for years blacks have made up a substantial majority of players in the league, the number of black coaches and front office people remains grossly disproportionately. Black players see this and believe that this is intentional. Of course the prerequisite for coaching and managing a football team is experience in and around the game". Those statements are very true to an extent. Today watching Kareem Abdul-Jabbar who was one of the best basketball players ever struggle to get a head-coaching job in the NBA is absurd, or is it? There is a stigma that is preventing him from getting an NBA coaching position. On the ownership issue it comes down to liquidity. Having the capital will make this act of ownership more realistic for anyone black or white.

A player that was denied ownership was the late Walter Payton. It makes me wonder why Mr. Payton was not given the chance to be an owner. He was wealthy, intelligent, well known, and a man of principles. That's probably the reason because most owners don't pride themselves on doing the right thing. Walter Payton's race hindered his chances of owning an NFL franchise and that's a complete shame because of the impact he's had on the game as a player and person. David Robinson is a great role model and I think he would be an excellent coach or owner. Certain black athletes have been plagued by social and racial problems that they have bestowed upon themselves. You just don't see white athletes receiving this type of media scrutiny or gaining these types of reputations. What if a well-known white athlete kills two black people one being his ex-wife? He would supposedly get off, right? How about NBA player Latrel Sprewell choking a white coach. You know if it were vice versa Jesse Jackson would get involved and demand it was a hate crime planned by David Duke. But Latrel gets a little slap on the wrist and eventually gets to continue playing. Those acts are prerequisites for going to jail. I don't have an ounce of prejudice in my body and this is not sour grapes. I am a man of unity and some of my closest friends are black and are like family to me. I wouldn't trade anything in the world for them, if it were not for some of them I wouldn't be the person I am today. O.J. Simpson. You decide. Maybe you already have.

The style of football played today is much different than it was three decades ago. It is a much more balanced attack. The passing has been perfected while by comparison to what it was thirty years ago. This means quicker scoring and games being decided by two-minute aerial attacks. The outcomes of games are not final until that last horn. Players like Michael Vick, Kurt Warner, and Marshall Faulk give the game so much excitement. Fans feel like they're watching a fast paced action thriller. The 2000 Super Bowl Champions St. Louis Ram's receiving core got nicknamed the fastest show on turf. Overall team speed of today's game versus thirty years ago is like a Porsche racing a Ford. Talent is so close that it takes a sharp-minded coach with consistent schemes to make the Super Bowl, which is the most exciting sporting event yearly in professional sports.

From Canada, to Amsterdam, from UK to Estero, Florida, football players have more chances to chase that never-ending boyhood dream. Opportunities to play three-decades ago were solely the NFL and the Canadian Football League which gave more American players a chance to play because CFL teams were located in the United States and Canada. While today the CFL is made up of only 9 teams that are located north of the United States border. Only a selected number of Americans get the invite to try to be the next Doug Flutie or Jeff Garcia. Most of these types of players are on the bubble of making NFL rosters or were exiled up there.

Then you have NFL-Europe, which is played from April to June throughout Western Europe, which is made up of six teams. This consists of players who were in the NFL and saw limited action, practice squad players, or guys who went to an NFL camp the year before and got released. Occasionally teams will allocate these types of players to Europe. Additional professional leagues are the Arena League (Chapter 16) and Arena League 2.

Politics has caused many athletes to lose faith, simply because many football personnel say one thing one day and something else the next. If there's little opposition they'll change where they stand overnight. For example when I was playing in Florida the day after final cuts were made. The coach became aware that a quarterback from his hometown area was released and immediately told the player to come down. When the player arrived, it was then they cut the backup quarterback. This move was done without even seeing the new quarter-back perform. When dealing with politics athletes are becoming more aware that coaches will say whatever it takes to get a player to sign with his team. They will even string a player along so another team won't be able to utilize their talents. These coaches are supposed to be the generals of professional football teams. Athletes have become so disenchanted by these acts that they lose the love for the game. Politics affect many people and often leave people standing in nearly dried cement, helpless with unanswered questions.

In the professional football market many athletes are very close in ability. Today with advanced technology in weight training, speed training, nutrition, and supplementation the game has been revolutionized. Nick Buoniconti, a former All-Pro linebacker for the 1973 Miami Dolphins, at 212 pounds played a key role in Miami's undefeated season. The 1974 Steelers offensive line averaged 247 pounds, while today Chicago Bears linebacker Brian Urlacher plays at 245 plus pounds and runs a 4.5 forty. The 2001 Super Bowl Champions Baltimore Ravens line averaged 310 pounds. In this era players are bigger, stronger, faster and much smarter about how they treat their bodies and deal with injuries. That Gladiator image that was portrayed in years past became extinct with the one bar facemasks and with the fact that eighty percent of the game was running the football.

The physical side of pro-football has changed tremendously in the past thirty years. Steroids have contributed to the success of many players and cannot only build muscle mass and strength but quickness and explosive speed. As a professional athlete you live a life of, money, publicity, girls and cars etc. This type of lifestyle will make just about anyone feel invincible. These players feel like they will never die or that life without football is death itself. Steroids are very harmful and if abused for a long time can cause severe health risks. Lyle Alzado was a star player for the Oakland Raiders. He was convinced that steroids were the leading factor of his terminal brain cancer that led to his death. With millions of dollars at stake to improve your forty-yard dash two-tenths of a second, just about any determined player might do a cycle of Winstrol-V, a water-based steroid given to horses to increase speed. Banned Olympic sprinter Ben Johnson tested positive for this type of drug in the 1988 Olympics in Seoul, Korea.

During the 1970's and up until 1987 steroids were legal in the NFL. Today they are banned, and if a player tests positive they will be suspended for the first four games, if tests positive a second time they will be suspended for six games and violating the rule a third time will lead to banishment from the NFL for a year with the right to an appeal after one year. Over time technology and advanced breakthroughs have enabled these players to beat the system. One of my closest friends and a current NFL player made it very aware to me that players today are abusing steroids even more than before. Players' salaries have skyrocketed in the past couple of decades, which enables players to hire chemists to create these drugs that are one or two molecules short of what the real drug is. This will still have the same effect but will not come up positive on the "piss test." Throughout all the levels of competitive sports I witnessed drug abuse first hand. The night after I played in a state All-Star game for football I was with four other athletes at a party. We left the party and parked on a trail in a secluded park. I was in the backseat when one of the kids took out an eight ball of cocaine and rolled up a dollar. They just started snorting. Thank God I had the will to say no. I saw exceptional athletic careers end that night. I was fortunate we didn't get pulled over by the police. The last I heard of those kids was two were in jail; one was in rehab and one overdosed. As a freshman in college I saw massive cocaine and alcohol consumption and even got offered to deal it. Throughout my collegiate and professional years I witnessed former teammates injecting themselves with steroids before competition and smoking weed like it was legal. I even had one teammate in the pros that used to blow cocaine on the bathroom sink before games. OxyContin, ecstasy and cocaine are examples of drugs that have destroyed some of my closest friendships. "A powerful medicine for pain, OxyContin has quickly become a dangerous street drug. According to the National Drug Intelligence Center, individuals in all age groups and social strata abuse OxyContin. There is no evidence that OxyContin abuse is particularly widespread among athletes, but doctors say that the drug could be beneficial to those competing through intense pain" (*Sports Illustrated, December 20, 2004*). There were times growing up I saw kids my age bulk up fast and it looked like all glory would be on them when the season started, gratefully the tables were turned. During my first year of college my priorities were not straight everyone makes mistakes and I am fortunate the mistakes I made did not ruin my career nor cost me my life. Ask yourself the question if millions of dollars were at stake and you could improve your forty-yard dash two tenths of a second would you take steroids? This question has entered my mind time and time again. It was not always easy to take the clean route however I am forever grateful for my parent's guidance and my own pure will to lead me into who I am today.

A starting NFL quarterback was averaging $1,470,000 in 1991, while in 2001, it increased to $3,829,000. A wide receiver was making $550,000 and today averages $2,114,000. Today NFL teams are worth around a billion dollars. The NFL is a league league where players can pick and choose which team they would like to play for through free agency.

With the media coverage and today's games being played in front of over 75,000 people the games put fans into football frenzies. Look at the Super Bowl for instance: households go crazy with Super Bowl parties and costumes. Next thing you know it will be declared a holiday. Established businesses with the finances are all about paying over a million dollars for a thirty second commercial. Is the NFL getting away from what the game really stands for or has dollar signs just completely restructured the game itself?

The salary cap is the amount each team can spend on its players each season. Created in 1994 the limit per team was thirty seven million. This amount is equivalent to sixty three percent of the leagues designated gross revenue. It's made up of television, radio, and gate receipts. Today it is up to seventy one point one million. This makes many players bitter because only the marquee players receive the big money. This is why free agency is common for many players because they can move around with plenty of options for more money. Between 1993–2001, 1,079 unrestricted free agents stayed and 1,177 moved on (NFLPA.org). Many veterans have to take large pay cuts which highly contributes towards them retiring. It seems like there is lack of loyalty with many organizations today. A prime example is Lawyer Milloy, a four time Pro Bowler and World Champion with the New England Patriots. He refused to take a pay cut and was released. In professional football, contracts don't mean to much. The only guaranteed money is the signing bonus, which is prorated over the years of the contract. I guess the smash mouth football and playing for the love of the game died with the four fathers of football, which were the players who played in 1910's, 1920's, 1930's and the 1940's.

There is a very small window of opportunity so when the chance comes athletes have to seize the moment. Many athletes, such as myself, have been blessed with the skills to play. But the one vital factor that will be missing is the opportunity. In my case that would mean being able to play the offensive specialist for a few games and show my ability or get into an NFL training camp. With lack of connections and a handful of second-rate sports agents not even someone of my caliber gets a realistic shot.

I might sound a little sour but I am speaking very hypothetically. There have been constant broken promises throughout my career. What ever happened to a righteous coach who really cares about the players? I think that must have ended when the Lombardi era did. Most come across as nice guys to the general public, but are different behind closed doors.

In the Arena 2 League most coaches bring in their own players from surrounding areas. The thing that really bothers me is that if a coach is unsuccessful one season it doesn't make sense why the next season he would not want to try some different combinations of players. That's a perfect example of the 2002 Carolina Rhino team. They were 2–14 and their team folded and their coach gets the defensive coordinating job with the Green Bay Blizzard and brings half his Carolina team to Green Bay. Being a very sincere, righteous person this entire distress is hard for me to cope with. In addition AF2 coaches have the complete say on talent and who's playing, unlike in the NFL when the general manager gets involved.

In Arena 2 football the majority of players all share the same dream of being the next poster boy, like Kurt Warner or Tommy Maddox. It all could be possible but it would be even more feasible with more league support. Don't get me wrong the league gives hundreds of players' opportunities to chase their dream but with an increase in pay I feel most players are going to sell out. With players being more productive and games getting more competitive and exciting, attendance will increase therefore revenue will far outweigh expenses.

Living conditions vary a great deal in Arena 2. Giving a player some extra benefits in college is cheating but how so in the pros. I think the league needs to be a little more flexible. In Florida I was staying at Montego Bay, which was an apartment complex with a pool, Jacuzzi's, tennis courts, weight room, washer, dryers and fully furnished apartments. It was very comfortable living conditions. Then in Carolina there were seven of us staying in a 3-bedroom, non-furnished apartment with roaches and people sleeping in closets. Norfolk was a hotel which was not bad, but when you're into eating healthily who wants to nuke your food daily. The league relies on the team to set up the housing for its players. This is where the league needs to step in and go into the cities where the teams are located and use their credibility to cut deals with apartment complexes or hotels to help get the players proper locations to reside.

Nutrition is another area overlooked by many organizations. Certain teams receive proper food deals while others are living like they're on "Survivor". Many athletes are uneducated from a nutrition standpoint about what is needed daily. By eating right and consuming the proper amount of calories the athlete is giving himself a competitive advantage. For instance, prior the week of a game I will usually really concentrate on my post recovery meal. After a hard three-hour practice I make sure that I am consuming high amounts of protein and carbohydrates. In addition sitting in a fifty-degree ice tube consistently after workouts is torture but it helps speed up your muscle recovery process. The protein will help repair the muscle and the complex carbohydrates will give me energy for the following night. The night before a game I would eat 16oz of pasta, which equals one pound. My teammates could not believe their eyes, but that gives me unlimited energy. In Florida, Louisville, Green Bay and Cincinnati, the players receive top-shelf pre-game meals. In Cincinnati, Chris Milon, former NFL running back was an assistant coach with the Swarm and owned his own restaurants so he took care of his players. While in Norfolk they distributed a Popeye's voucher to eat, which was a free two-piece dinner with the purchase of a soft drink. On the other hand in Memphis this team feeds you two solid meals daily not to mention the duplex you reside in is very upscale, and was also a gated community with a pool, workout room, and tennis courts.

God has given me firsthand experience to become a sincere and honorable coach. The unfortunate things that I have encountered are issues I will try to avoid as a coach. I will be a coach for the player who needs a break and is one opportunity away from finding his niche and fulfilling his or her dream.

15

THE FORTY-YARD DASH: $$

"With out dreams there is no reason to sleep."

—**Anonymous**

In the United States there is around 15,000 high school football teams with an estimated 983,600 football players participating in the fall throughout the country and 281,000 being seniors. Texas alone has 1,193 high school football teams, while Alaska has less then 20 teams. The small state of Massachusetts has 275 plus teams. According to Todd Petr of the NCAA research team 60,000 college athletes from over 624 football programs ranging from all NCAA levels, covering fifty different states participated in college football for the 2004 season.

Division I consists of 25,000, Division II, 14,000 and Division III has 20,000 players. In reference to the NCAA 5.8% of High School football players go on to play college (NCAA.org). The NFL keeps files on almost all players but only actively scout 6,000. From that group, 340 are invited to the annual scouting combine held in Indianapolis. Less than 1,000 players coming out of college signed contracts with NFL clubs, and from that group, just over 330 will make a club roster. If past precedents prevail fewer than 150 of those players will remain in the NFL after four seasons (NFLPA.org). An estimated 20,600 seniors finish their college careers yearly. The NFL through the draft, which consists of 7 rounds, will select 262 players, which is less than 1%.

As of 2001, 573 un-drafted rookie free agents signed. In 1990, the first round picks average salary was $850,000 with a signing bonus of 1,335,000. While in 2001, the average salary for this type of player was $1,700,000 and the signing bonus was $3,817,000. Each year the NFL employs over 1,800 players, NFL-Europe 252, CFL 324, AFL 436, and AF2 546. There are approximately 3,358 professional football players playing yearly. Out of that number there are rookies, unrestricted and restricted free agents. CFL rosters can only sign seventeen American players per CFL Team, and there are only nine CFL teams. The NFL Europe has six teams with forty-two players, with seven being international players. All these above referenced players are in this pool. Looking back I feel very privileged to be one of 3,358 out of over twenty thousand seniors to play after college and the thousands of free agents looking for work. Only a small percentage of those who graduate from college make it to a professional football level.

To narrow down all these players and dictate who has the ability to play at the professional level players must master the forty-yard dash. Fast forty times during combines or pro-days will almost guarantee a player a realistic look from the NFL. This is where a player can raise or lower his status tremendously by a couple of hundredths of a second. The most important test in football, is the forty-yard dash. This could lead to large sums of money (in the millions) for signing bonus, a roster spot, or college scholarship. For example say if a wide receiver from University of Montana ends his collegiate career with only fifteen catches but runs a 4.31 in his pro-day his chances to sign, as a free agent will increase greatly. Is that fair when a receiver from Holy Cross ends his career with over 300 catches and 50 touchdown's and tests out at a 4.78. No, but that's the nature of the business, especially if that 4.7 player has complete game speed and runs textbook routes. I have played with some complete burners when it comes to testing out on the forty but can't catch a cold and just don't possess the football savvy.

How do you run the forty-yard dash? Do you know how to start? Breathe? Finish? Do you know what shoes to wear to lower your time? Do you know how long your first step should be? Which foot you should put forward at the start? Clock tense up is when a player runs fast forties on his own but when he runs in front of the scouts he tightens up and his mind is all over the place. I can relate to this pretty well. Ron used to clock me at 4.48s and I would test out at some pro workouts at 4.6s.

Occasionally a player that is an inconsistent forty runner will fall through the cracks and make it to the NFL level. Jerry Rice is a legitimate 4.65. Too much stock goes into the 40-yard dash. How many times in a game does a player run forty yards straight without any equipment? There are many excellent football players who are held back because of the forty-yard dash. In addition running a 4.4 to a 4.7 the difference is inches. If you add them up that could be what separates a player from making that game-winning run or a receiver creating the separation to make the tough catch.

With all of these players coming out of college the scouts need something to narrow down the talent or every player in America would feel that they are getting denied the chance of living that dream and playing in the NFL.

16

IRON MAN FOOTBALL: INSIDE THE ARENA

"The ultimate measure of a man is not where he stands in moments of comfort and convenience, but where he stands at times of challenge, and controversy."

—Martin Luther King Jr.

According to AFL history on <u>arenafootball.com</u>, in February of 1981 an NFL marketing expert, James F. Foster outlined a miniaturized football field over a hockey rink. He sketched this miniature football field on an envelope while watching the Major Indoor Soccer League All-Star Game at Madison Square Garden. Twenty something years later Arena football has evolved into one of the most electrifying brands of professional football. With the NFL being a monopoly, Foster realized that there was no room for competition. This is why he decided to create an indoor, summer "hybrid." I personally believe that if the creator of XFL, Vince McMahon didn't try to compete with the NFL, the XFL would have lasted.

Foster applied the best of the outdoor game to the AFL with modern twists. The field measures eighty-five feet wide and fifty yards long with eight-yard end zones. Goal posts are smaller then the NFL's and measures nine feet wide with a crossbar height of fifteen feet (NFL goal posts are eighteen and a half feet wide with the crossbar at ten feet). The goal-side rebound nets are thirty feet wide by thirty feet high. The name Arena Football goes without saying, the game is played inside of an Arena, which is a positive. The weather is always the same comfortable atmosphere. Not worrying about Mother Nature's ability to affect games is a major perk for the sport. Neither players nor fans have to worry about battling the heat of the summer, or the cold brisk weather in the winter. This ensures that every game will be comfortable and that fans will show up no matter No matter what the weather is outside. Being a skilled player with speed the weather can play a key role in your success. Wet surfaces, rain, snow, cold, stiff muscles, humidity are never concerns of an Arena Football player. However there is a down side to this perfect inside atmosphere, the sideline boards, lighting and the surface that the games are played on. Fans have lower costs to attend an Arena game. A family can attend an Arena game for far less than an NFL game. A family of four can go to an Arena game for $42.00. It would cost a family of four $180.00 to watch an NFL game. Your entertainment value of Arena football is more exhilarating because the pace the game is played at and the intimacy between the fan and the player.

Sideline barriers are also known as the infamous walls. These walls are made of high-density foam rubber and stand 48 inches high. These foam boards are also used as advertisements for companies, which was a great idea to bring revenue into the league. Even though they are made out of foam and look soft, boy does it hurt when you get tackled into them or even over one of them. After playing my first game on this field in front of crowd I quickly realized that this in-door field was much quicker and faster then the outdoor game I was accustom too.

As a player, it is a difficult adjustment to get used to the lighting inside the Arenas. It is especially hard during games if you are a rookie and you do not practice in the Arena everyday. Making the transition from playing outside into the Arena was difficult for me at first. In Florida we only had a couple of practices inside during preseason due to the fact that we shared the Arena with the Pro-Hockey team the Florida Everglades. While playing for the Louisville Fire we were able to practice the majority of the time inside the Arena, which helped me get used to the lighting. With the Memphis Xplorers, my second season, we practiced inside every night. This is where my arena skills really developed and I was awarded the teams most improved player. As a player once you have time to adjust to the lighting the atmosphere is perfect. What more could a football player ask for, perfect weather every game.

One negative about the Arena League is the surface that the games are played on, astro-turf. Astro-turf is basically a grass rug over concrete, and let me tell you first hand that it feels like concrete when you get tackled on it. It's known for the wears and tears that contribute to the players aching bodies. From the collegiate to the pro level numerous organizations are doing away with this surface and are installing synthetic grass. I believe that astro-turf contributes to a faster exit from football than if playing on grass. However simply because astro-turf does not require the same care as real grass, it saves organizations thousands of dollars. I guess saving money is more important than the longevity of players careers. The game is becoming more of a revolving door because of the fast turnover rate. They figure that there are hundreds of other players waiting for their opportunity. I believe that Arena football should do away with astro-turf and put in synthetic grass. This will enable franchises to utilize these iron men players to the extreme and possibly lengthen their careers.

The equipment that Arena Football players wear differs from player to player. Through all levels, preceding the professional level, football players must wear all lower pads to protect hips, thighs and knees. However at the professional level you can wear what lower pads you feel are needed. I never wore any of my lower pads playing Arena Football do to how much more explosive I felt when I didn't wear them. I also did not wear your traditional turf shoes while playing Arena Football. I chose to wear light track shoes to enable me to be as versatile as I could. I wore Nike Zooms one and a half sizes to small, which left me feeling light on my feet feeling as if I were only wearing slippers. The football game itself is very fast and quick inside the Arena and trust me, you want to be as explosive as you can when you are out on that field. The Arena football helmet is a little bigger and made with more cushioning then the traditional football helmet. It is manufactured to try to reduce the impact your head takes when hitting the turf and wall.

Surprising to many, the official AFL football is the same size and weight as the NFL's football. The only difference is that the AFL football does not have any white on it and the coloring is different. The ball in Arena football is made out of two different shades of dark leather. I believe that the two different shades was applied to help the players see the ball with the inside lighting. However it is a hard adjustment to keep your eye on the ball with the lighting inside the Arena. It is also an adjustment to keep your eye on the ball without any white on the ball. The lighting is very bright so you really have to focus when the ball was thrown your way.

In Arena Football there is an eight-player single platoon system with a 24-man active roster. Players play offense and defense with the exception of the kicker, quarterback, offensive specialist (the kick returner on defense), and two defensive specialists. Four offensive players must line up on the line of scrimmage. Three defensive players must be down linemen (in a three point stance). One linebacker may blitz on either side of the center. Alignment is two yards off the line of scrimmage. Offensive motion consists of one receiver that may go in forward motion before the snap. Time restrictions consist of fifteen-minute quarters with a fifteen-minute halftime. The clock stops for out-of-bounds plays or incomplete passes only in the last minute of each half or when the referee signals a penalty, injured player, or timeout (www.arenafootball.com). Four downs are allowed to advance the ball ten yards for a first down or to score. Six points for a touchdown, one point for a conversion by place kick after a touchdown, two points for a drop kick, two points for a run or pass after a touchdown, three points for a field-goal and two points for a safety.

Kickoffs take place from the goal line. Kickers have the option to use a one-inch tee. Shockingly punting is considered illegal. On fourth down, a team may go for a first down, touchdown, or field goal. The receiving team may field any kickoff or missed field goal that rebounds off the net. Any kickoff untouched, which is out of bounds, will be placed at the 20-yard line or the place where it went out of bounds; whichever is more helpful to the receiving team. Passing rules are the same as NCAA Football in which receivers must have one foot inbounds. A unique exception in Arena football is the rebound nets. A forward pass that rebounds off of the end zone net is a live ball and is in play until it touches the playing surface. This rule alone makes it a much faster game then the outside version, with players rushing to the live ball. Each overtime period is fifteen minutes during the regular season and playoffs. Each team gets one possession to score. If, after each team has had one possession, one team is ahead, that team wins. If the teams are tied after each has had a possession, the next team to score wins.

After the rise and fall of the United States Football League in 1985, Foster began to further re-create the game. To get a feel for how the public would react he conducted a "test game" in Rockford, Illinois, on April 26, 1986. The response led to a "showcase game" the following year in Chicago. That game was greeted by 8,200 fans and smoothed the way for the national debut of the AFL in 1987. In 1987 the inaugural season, four teams made up the league. These teams were: Chicago Bruisers, Denver Dynamite, Pittsburgh Gladiators, and Washington Commandos. The average attendance during the inaugural season was around 11,279. That year, live on ESPN, the Dynamite won Arena Bowl I in front of 13,232 fans. Detroit Dive, Dallas Texans, and Albany Firebirds joined the league the following season (www.arenafootball.com).

A new era was created three years later in 1990, with "The 50-Yard Indoor War." Foster along with his partners made the decision to sell licenses to investors in major markets and thereby enable private ownership of teams. On March 27, 1990, U.S. Patent Office issued patent No. 4,911,433 for the Arena Football

Game System, making it the only sports league in history able to play a patented rival-free game. In the year 1991 the league expanded from six to eight teams. These teams included: Orlando Predators. Another sun-belt team, the Tampa Bay Storm (formerly the Pittsburgh Gladiators), This team set a single game record with 24,445 fans. For that season until that point the all-time attendance recorded was around 12,813 fans per game (www.arenafootball.com). The Arizona Rattlers were introduced into the Arena Football world in 1992. The following season the Rattlers and Predators sold-out each home game.

In the year 1995, the Iowa Barnstormers, quarterbacked by current NFL and Super Bowl M.V.P. Kurt Warner fell eight points short of an Arena Bowl IX appearance. The following year in 1996 the fan total reaches 1 million per season. The following year in 1997 the league was run by a 14-team circuit and was averaging nearly 16,000 fans per game. Four new teams were introduced: the Nashville Cats, New Jersey Red Dogs, New York City Hawks, and Portland Foreast Dragons. As each year passed the Arena Football League was catching more attention as well as adding new teams.

The Arena Football League began its 13th season and eclipsed the one million mark for the third straight season. Two million viewers watched the Arena Bowl XII make its first appearance on ABC. According to a 1998 ESPN Chilton Sports poll, Arena Football was named as one of the "newest sports" that emerged in the U.S. over the last 10 years (www.arenafootball.com). On February 8, 1999, the Arena League joined alliances with the NFL. The NFL agreed to purchase an exclusive option to obtain an equity interest in the AFL. The option could be exercised over the next 18 months and would give the NFL a minority ownership interest (up to 49.9%) in the AFL and a say in the operation of the league (subject to approval of the NFL owners).

The first NFL owner approved by the AFL Board of Directors was New Orleans Saints owner Tom Benson to host a team in the "Big Easy." Before this rule, NFL owners were prohibited from investing or owning other football leagues or teams. On August 24, 1999, the AFL Board of Directors announced that Arena football 2-the AFL's triple-A would begin play in April 2000. Fifteen teams ranging from midsize cities in the Southeast and Midwest made up the inaugural season. The AF2 league has had a positive image of helping players utilize their talents to move up the ladder of professional football. The skill level is very impressive and consistent. In 2002, 30 teams made up the AF2. The AF2 serves as a vehicle to bring Arena Football to second-tier cities. AF2 is full of players who slipped through the cracks, says AF2 Executive Director Jerry Kurz. "Maybe they attended a small school and went unnoticed, or maybe they have not reached the peak of their potential. Whatever the situation, AF2 is providing an opportunity for these athletes to continue their maturation process as professional football players. In 2004 over thirty former AF2 players spent time on rosters in the NFL and CFL. AF2 operates under the same mission statement and Fan's Bill or Rights as the Arena Football League. (www.arenafootball.com). In addition Canada was getting its first taste of live Arena football in Toronto. That year more than 2.5 million fans watched Arena Football.

Today Arena Football is hotter than ever, with a 17-team circuit. This is truly iron man football, what I mean by that is it takes a versatile player to be an arena player. "Not every NFL player could play in the Arena League and that is not just coming from a former player but from a future NFL Hall of Fame player, Warren Sapp. Sapp was interviewed during an Arena game and was asked to comment on it: "This is strictly an athlete's game. I wouldn't be able to survive playing both sides of the ball." Current Green Bay Packer Receiver and former AFL player Antonio Chatman states: "They say that the NFL is a step faster than college." I would say Arena is a step faster than the NFL because of the size of the field in Arena. And the players too: there are players in the Arena League that could excel in the NFL" (arenafootball.com). Players will opt to stay in the states then head north. Due to the NFL's impact and games being televised on NBC the leagues stock and credibility has greatly increased. Kurt Warner, Tommy Maddox, and David Patten, were former AFL players and are current NFL stars. Many critics are trying to determine what made these three players have such a smooth transition to the NFL (www.arenafootball.com).

The most well known player of these three is Kurt Warner, a former Northern Iowa star. Numerous NFL teams passed him by. Warner made the condensed Arena game a time to sharpen his skills. Quick releases, passing, precise 3 to 5 step drops made Warner that much more accurate in threading the needle. The same goes for Tommy Maddox, the 2002 NFL's comeback player of the year who had a stint with the New Jersey Red Dogs. Next on the list is former Albany Firebird "lighting in a bottle" and current World Champion wide receiver New England Patriot David Patten. Patten has exceptional quickness and footwork and gets in and out of his routes very quickly. He credits his time in the AFL for fully developing his wide receiver skills. As competition gets even fiercer it will be interesting to see if released players from the NFL can make the adjustments from the 100 yard field to the miniature size one. Many receivers find it hard to adjust to the 9th man in the Arena, the wall.

Multiplicity is a key component to Arena football. The more you can do the better. Receivers have three classifications in the Arena League. The primary receiver is the offensive specialist who gets 75 % of the balls. Then their is the 'Z', or the secondary receiver who works off the offensive specialist as the number two pass option; he's usually the two-way player who plays defensive back also. Thirdly, there is the backside (X) receiver who is used for slants, crosses and hitches; they play the 'jack' on defense. A non-blitzing linebacker sits in a 5–5 box and eyes the tight end to fullback. On defense there are two defensive specialists. The game is very offense oriented and 96 % of the game is passing.

In AF2 there are many rules that differ from conventional football thus making the game that much more fast paced and thrilling. Excitement and the dedication of the fans in Arena Football is simply remarkable. Down south this game is as popular as the outdoor game, and the Arena is filled to the capacity. Pregame was a period when I got my adrenaline going, and the most excited to play. Running into the Arena and being introduced is something that I will always remember. At first when the teams are introduced the Arena is in complete darkness, with Harleys revving up their engines, fire truck sirens blaring, fireworks being set off and bright flames coming out of the tunnel we ran through. To be introduced made the game even more intense and made the fans go wild. It made me feel like we were getting introduced to play in the Super Bowl every game. During the games the fans went wild and got really into the game.

When a player scored a touchdown, they were sure to do a dance in the end zone that made the crowd go crazy. We got a few good laughs with some of the dances the players came out with after they scored a touchdown. Each time television cut out for a commercial a representative from the home team would come and randomly select a few fans to compete for a chance to win all different types of prizes. During these television breaks team representatives also walked around with enormous sling shots and sling t-shirts into specific areas of the Arenas that make the most noise. This period puts fans back into their youth by engaging them in acts that they don't often perform. One example is a forty-year-old man running in a circle bent over with his forehead on a baseball bat. After ten spins he has to try to kick a field goal.

After each home game some teams in the league have player's auction off a home jersey for the fans. The money made during the auction was donated to charities. There are also autograph sessions for the fans after games on the field. During autograph sessions in Louisville we had a couple of concerts with up and coming singing sensations, which made the crowd go absolutely wild. The capacity of an Arena ranges from approximately eight thousand to eighteen thousand. Usually the Arena is filled and gets very loud with cheering, which rushes your adrenaline. However if you're a member of an opposing team the fans are not on your side and they make it well known when you first step into the Arena. If you go over the side barriers and don't get a beer shower on your head or a hot dog thrown at you, consider yourself lucky.

Arena Football is stronger than ever today. Fun, exciting family oriented and affordable has helped this sport grow in the last couple of decades. Savvy league officials have implemented different marketing and business techniques that have boosted revenues. One team I was involved with the general manager made it clear to certain players that he was putting a bounty on the opponents quarterback and if they knocked him out of the game an envelope would be sitting in their locker with some Ben Franklins in it. I felt that this behavior was going to the extreme, but some individuals will go to the extreme to win.

Within the AFL2 there is talent through the league with exceptional players. However there is also hidden talent in the league with players hanging on and waiting to get their opportunity to shine and be discovered. For example my good friend Ryan Russell defines a diamond in the rough. He has tremendous speed and is probably the most explosive player I have seen for his size. Ryan should be returning kicks and punts for an NFL team today but is in quest of getting the opportunity. Mike Summers had over three hundred tackles throughout his collegiate career. He is a very physical and athletic defensive back with the skills to play at the highest level. Nick Johnson is pound for pound the best football player I have ever played with. Standing at about 5'6". He has no fear and is just as talented artist/magician as a football player. He would not hesitate to go head to head with 300-pound player. His size has completely hindered his chances of moving up the ladder of professional football. However the Arena league has given him the opportunity to play at the professional level. Nick Johnson stated, "Arena football was made for quick people who are vertically challenged. I feel to many pro athletes get mixed up in the wild life. I have played with guys who have a wife and a baby at home and a girlfriend on the road. I call them a sponsor someone who supports the athlete with sex, money and a car. In the AF2 players receive all the fame and hype as the NFL. The only difference is the zeros at the end of the paycheck." Nick started with Wayne Chrebet at Hofstra. "We were playing Delaware and Wayne scored his fifth touchdown to tie Jerry Rice's record. After he scored his third on the same defensive back they put his twin brother in and Wayne scored his forth and fifth touchdown of the game on him. He earned his spot in the NFL. Arena football is an excellent springboard for football players to move up to the NFL. This league enables players to showcase their skills so they can get more of a realistic look to continue their career at a higher level.

17

LIFE IT'S OKAY TO DREAM

✦

4TH AND INCHES

"Cherish yesterday, Dream tomorrow, Live today."

—Anonymous

I looked up the word dream in the Webster Dictionary and it read: i: series of thoughts, images, or emotions occurring during sleep ii: an experience of waking life having the characteristics of a dream: a visionary creation of the imagination.

At times I get really caught up in my dream and in the game of football. There are times that I have to remind myself that football is just a game. A couple times a month I will have a dream relating to football, that I am getting ready to play in my first NFL game. The dream feels so realistic and leaves me saddened when I awaken. A day does not go by when I do not think about football. Even after being a part of three championship teams and winning some prestigious awards I feel my signature moment came when I threw a Hail Mary pass against Winthrop with no time left on the clock. If that didn't occur our team would not have won a championship that year. I wish my signature moment happened towards the end of my career. I consider that my signature moment, but not my greatest achievement. Being selected to the All-New England Teams in both football and basketball in prep school would rank at the top of my athletic achievements, especially after being overlooked as an All-Scholastic athlete my senior year at Salem High. In the greater loop of life football can't compare to family and being healthy. It is funny how things work out and you find yourself doing something different than you have ever dreamed of doing. I guess that one dream has a way of leading to another. I am reminded daily by my parents and Krista that I did indeed beat the odds and made it to the professional level.

I have faced detours along my journey and I can honestly say that I made the most out of all my opportunities. I think that Al Pochino said it best in *Any Given Sunday*, "Football is a game of inches". It is like a puzzle, there are many pieces that go into it and if you're missing one it will never get finished. I have never blamed anyone for the road I had to travel to get to where I am, nor will I ever. Certain people who held me back may have felt they controlled my destiny by deterring me, however they actually helped me become more determined to go after my dream and to be successful in life.

I was at college in Poughkeepsie, New York (55 minutes north from NYC) when the attacks occurred at the World Trade Center. It was devastating and depressing; words cannot describe the feelings I had. Each night before bed I would see families holding pictures of their loved ones up asking if anyone has seen this person and to please call the hot line. Anytime you think you have problems, go to Ground Zero. Bodies perished, dreams died and children became orphaned. Each year Krista and I take a trip out to New York City. When we walk by Ground Zero there is an emptiness that fills the air, it is overwhelming and saddens us. A survivor of Tower 1 once told me about his tragic story. "I was on the 85th floor when the plane hit and where I was located I saw the plan coming right at the building. It felt like the building was going to tip into the Hudson. It took me seventy minutes to reach the bottom and minutes later the entire building came down. The courage the firefighters displayed was overwhelming. I think they new they were walking to there deaths. Even to this day when I hear thunder my body shakes. I am psychologically beaten for the rest of my life." Thank God that America has the men and women of the armed forces. They are the true heroes and make it possible for people like myself to go out and live the American dream. I don't think that I could ever thank these soldiers enough and pray for their safety daily.

The NFL as well as the AFL prides itself on community service and giving back to the community. I was fortunate enough to visit St. Jude's Children's Hospital in Memphis, Tennessee. Before I walked into the hospital I was nervous to see children suffering from disease, however I was filled with joy to brighten their day. As we walked into the activities area where we met the children from all over the country who were suffering from cancer, the room was filled with smiles and life. It was then I knew that I would never be the same and viewed life from a different perspective. I saw children so ill with cancer in wheelchairs fighting for their lives hoping for a miracle. It was touching for me to bring joy to their life by giving my autograph. There was one girl I will always hold close my heart. Here name was Brittany; she was a fourteen-year-old girl who had been fighting cancer for five years. She had one of the rarest cancers that no one had ever beaten and was restricted to a wheelchair. Brittany barely has any hair left, but kept a beautiful smile that shows off her big blue eyes. She told us that one day she hoped that she could become a cheerleader for the University of Tennessee; she kept her dream alive even though she was fighting a life threatening disease. I walked into the hospital thinking that I was there to inspire these children and brighten there day; however they are the ones who inspired me. I only hope that I can give back to them what they gave to me and that is why I donate money to that hospital annually. I wish that I could give more to these children and pray for a miracle for each and every one of them.

One of my teammates at Marist College was J.J Allen. He was an inspiration to all that knew him. He lost his battle with cancer this past year. Prior to the start of my sophomore season I was ready to walk away from football because of personal problems. J.J convinced me I would regret it and gave me a quote I live by today "Are you better than you were yesterday." I will hold his memories in my heart. He too will forever be in my prayers. In November 1998, I was at college and my father called me and revealed Big Al Cicco passed away. He was a fan of mine and was the mouth of our neighborhood. It was a total shock and really put everything in my life into perspective, especially of how great it is to have such a wonderful family.

Many of us take too much for granted and don't understand things can be taken away from us in a matter of seconds. I see people at malls and supermarkets fussing over parking spaces that are closer to the entrances. I say: park in the back once in a while and enjoy the walk because there are people restricted to wheelchairs that would kill to make that walk. What do you think Brittany would give to be able to have the strength to make that walk? I used to worry about what I didn't have and what I haven't done, but not anymore, I am grateful.

Whether it's becoming a lawyer, doctor, or pro-football player, anything is possible if you put your mind and heart to it. We live in the greatest country in the world that offers us the proper resources to succeed in whatever careers we decide to pursue. Football has taken me places that I would have never gone. But it has also given me an education no other curriculum could offer. My best advice to parents whose children want to play professionally is always think education first. In order to succeed at the professional level of anything you have to stay true to your priorities, sacrifice like no other and want to succeed more than anything.

This has added to my human capital and has helped me realize that when you follow one dream it leads to another.

People have compared my work ethic to Jerry Rice, a person I respect as a player. This is a player that is the best at what he does. I look forward to carrying that asset into the sports agent profession.

This book was not written to target athletes alone but to ordinary people, people like myself who have a dream and realize that their time on this earth is limited. If you are willing to put yourself and your dreams on the line, in the worst case you will discover an inner strength you might not have known existed. Like Krista has told me time and time again: "Always believe in your family and yourself, never lose your faith." Most importantly, don't be afraid to fail because you will never know what your limitations are until you take that chance. I hope my journey has been an inspiration and has moved many. Always remember "Without Dreams there is no reason to Sleep." I would like to give a special thanks to *The Prayer of Jabez* for giving me the guidance mentally to be able to live a blessed life when my skies were looking very gray.

Krista has been a dream come true and blessing from above. We are fortunate to have each other to go through the ups and downs of life together. I am looking forward to starting my life with her as my wife. My brothers are both my best friends and have been there for me since before I can remember. I will cherish the memories we have shared.

Many people don't know how special their parents are, I have been able to experience their unconditional love and support first hand. I wanted to make it to the NFL not only to fulfill my dream but to also take care of my parents and loved ones. My father has made tremendous sacrifices from day one and always made sure he gave me every opportunity to be successful in life. I don't think that I could ever thank my mother enough for being the glue that held our family together.

When I was getting bounced around by teams it would have been very easy for me to become bitter and walk away from my dream, but I believed in myself and kept battling, and that makes my journey worth telling. This manuscript might be finished, but my journey is far from complete.

978-0-595-34231-0
0-595-34231-0

Printed in the United States
142214LV00009B/49/A

9 780595 342310